Alpine Wildflowers

Showy Wildflowers of the Alpine and Subalpine Areas of the Rocky Mountain States.

photography and text by
Dr. Dee Strickler

illustration and graphic design by
Zoe Strickler-Wilson

Front Cover: Buttercup Family *(Ranunculaceae)*

COLORADO COLUMBINE, Blue Columbine
Aquilegia coerulea James

Note: For a description see page 74.

Library of Congress Catalog Card 89-82747
ISBN 1-56044-011-2

Published by The Flower Press
Columbia Falls, Montana

Publishing Consultant:
Falcon Press Publishing Co., Inc.,
Helena and Billings, Montana

To order extra copies of this book, contact:
The Flower Press, 192 Larch Lane, Columbia Falls, MT 59912, or
Falcon Press, P.O. Box 1718, Helena, MT 59624
or call toll-free 1-800-582-2665.

Printed in Singapore.

First printing 1990
Second printing 1991
Third printing 1993

Acknowledgements

The author owes a debt of gratitude to numerous people for help in plant identification, proofreading and other assistance in the preparation of this book. Special thanks and appreciation are extended to Dr. Jeanette Oliver, botanist at Flathead Valley Community College, Kalispell, Montana; to Kathy Ahlenslager, Department of Botany, University of Montana, Missoula; to Peter Lesica, rare plant specialist, Missoula, Montana and to Peter Stickney, USDA Forest Service, Missoula, for help in identifying species and for other generous help.

I wish also to recognize the kind assistance of Joy Mastrogiuseppe, Department of Botany, Washington State University, Pullman, Washington.

My daughter Zoe Strickler-Wilson contributed substantially with the graphic design and art work.

Finally, I thank my wife, Claire, for patient help in picture selection, for help with the manuscript and for constant support and encouragement.

—Whitefish, Montana, December, 1989

About the author

Dee Strickler is a Wood Scientist and Technologist holding a B.S. from Washington State University, M.S. from Syracuse University and a doctorate from Duke University. His forestry undergraduate curriculum included a minor in botany. As Wood Technologist on the College of Engineering Faculty of Washington State University for many years, he authored over 50 technical publications and reports on original research in the fields of wood properties and glued wood products.

Dr. Strickler has enjoyed wildflower photography for more than 20 years and herein shares that interest and enjoyment with others.

Contents

Introduction 5
Map of Rocky Mountain States 8
Lily Family *(Liliaceae)* 9
Parsley Family *(Apiaceae, Umbelliferae)* 14
Sunflower Family *(Asteraceae, Compositae)* 16
Borage Family *(Boraginaceae)* . . . . 27, Back Cover
Mustard Family *(Brassicaceae, Cruciferae)* 30
Harebell Family *(Campanulaceae)* 32
Pink Family *(Caryophyllaceae)* 34
Stonecrop Family *(Crassulaceae)* 37
Heath Family *(Ericaceae)* 38
Pea Family *(Fabaceae, Leguminosae)* 41
Bleeding Heart Family *(Fumariaceae)* 46
Gentian Family *(Gentianaceae)* 46
Gooseberry Family *(Grossulariaceae)* 52
Waterleaf Family *(Hydrophyllaceae)* 53
St. Johnswort Family *(Hypericaceae)* 54
Mint Family *(Labiatae)* 54
Bladderwort Family *(Lentibulariaceae)* 55
Evening Primrose Family *(Onagraceae)* 56
Phlox Family *(Polemoniaceae)* 58
Poppy Family *(Papaveraceae)* 59
Wild Buckwheat Family *(Polygonaceae)* 61
Purslane Family *(Portulacaceae)* 65
Primrose Family *(Primulaceae)* 67
Buttercup Family *(Ranunculaceae)* . . . . 70, Front Cover
Rose Family *(Rosaceae)* 80
Saxifrage Family *(Saxifragaceae)* 87
Figwort Family *(Scrophulariaceae)* 92
Valerian Family *(Valerianaceae)* 104
Violet Family *(Violaceae)* 104
Selected References 105
Glossary 106
Index 108
On Photographing Wildflowers 111

Introduction

Alpine Wildflowers is the third volume of guide books on the showy wildflowers of the northern Rocky Mountain states. The series began with *Prairie Wildflowers,* 1986, followed by *Forest Wildflowers,* 1988.

These guide books help hikers, outdoorsmen, travelers, amateur botanists and all lovers of nature who want to know "What flower is that?" Professional botanists and range managers will find them a helpful supplement to more authoritative works on the flora of the northern Rockies. School teachers and students from elementary schools to universities will also use them as beginner's guides to botany and wildflower appreciation.

The flowers in this book appear in family sequence. The system of grouping flowers by color is not used, because wide color variations frequently occur within a single species, often causing as much confusion as help to the amateur.

For each flower pictured, some of the most noticeable features of the species are described, including the leaves, blooming period, habitat and range in which the plant grows. Some pertinent comments of general interest about the species or family may also be included. The flowers shown in this or any similar guide can only include a sample of the seemingly endless array in our natural world. The comments pertaining to individual flowers in the text frequently mention other closely related species that one may encounter. An attempt was made to include at least one species from each family and each major genus of showy wildflowers commonly found in the alpine flora of the northern Rockies. The author hopes that he has achieved a fair balance and that everyone can discover beauty and pleasure among these pages.

Most of the alpine terrain in our region rests in federal ownership and much of it lies within various wilderness areas. Other portions are in national parks such as Glacier, Yellowstone, Teton, and Rocky Mountain. Still other alpine heights are within national forests. Consequently, much of our alpine lands are accessible to the public but only by hiking trails or on horseback. Highways that do cross alpine passes include those in Glacier Park, the Beartooth Range in Montana and Wyoming, the Bighorn and Medicine Bow ranges in Wyoming, the high Uinta Mountains of Utah and Rocky Mountain National Park, among numerous high passes, in Colorado. Thus anyone can enjoy our alpine flora by automobile if they chose to do so.

Alpine Wildflowers

Most alpine plants are dwarfed by harsh environmental conditions, particularly low temperatures and strong winds. Many of them grow close to the ground in mats or cushions. They must be hardy enough to withstand hard frosts, even during the blooming period.

Perennials predominate in the alpine flora, because the growing season is short and few annuals can complete their life cycles during one short season. Many alpine flowers display intense colors. Large, full sized blossoms often occur even on dwarfed plants. Many colorful flowers in the alpine flora with pleasing fragrances readily attract pollenizing insects in the rush to complete the regeneration cycle in a short time.

High altitude and high latitude have much the same effect on plant growth. Many plants common to the arctic regions of the northern hemisphere extend their ranges south in the high mountains where growing conditions are similar to the arctic.

Some alpine plants also grow at lower elevations as well. By traveling upward at the right season of the year, one can find all stages in the life cycle of such species, from the mature seed stage on the plains or lower mountains to springtime budding at alpine heights. Still other plant families have developed species that thrive only at high elevation. They have adapted their life cycles for survival only in the alpine environment.

The main alpine flower display occurs in June and July and it is often spectacular. It coincides with the period of maximum daylight. By late August the alpine summer virtually ends. Mosquitoes can be bothersome early in the alpine season, but their numbers usually diminish by midsummer.

The Alpine Environment

Alpine is usually defined as the treeless region in high mountains above timberline. Rocky or gravelly terrain generally prevails. Grasses and sedges form thick but fragile sod in meadows and the sparse soil of the less steep slopes. The name tundra applies here as well as in the arctic. Alpine soils are typically sparse because of severe erosion from wind, water, and glaciers. Flowering plants must therefore send down strong roots to find limited soil nutrients and moisture.

Subalpine is an intermediate zone between montane or mountain forests and treeless alpine expanses. Forests of Engelmann Spruce and subalpine fir predominate, but pines with five-needle clusters and a few other tree species also occur. These subalpine timber stands commonly grow in patches with open meadows or parks in between. The trees become stunted and distorted on the more exposed sites. The German word "krummholz" applies to such trees, meaning bent, crooked or elfin wood—literally translated "crummy timber."

The subalpine flora begins at about 6,000 to 6,500 feet elevation in northern Idaho and northwestern Montana, but around 9,000 to 10,500 feet in Colorado and northern Utah. Winter snows normally stay late in the subalpine areas and melting snow keeps streambanks and rivulets watered throughout most of the summer.

Spring may come early to exposed alpine ridges and slopes where wind blows most of the snow away. The snow blows into drifts in cirques and draws where spring may come very late or not at all. Spring generally comes later in the subalpine than in the alpine zone, because snow stays later in areas protected by subalpine forests.

6

Picking or transplanting of wildflowers is strictly discouraged in the high mountains. Some species are rare or even endangered and indiscriminate removal could lead to extinction. Numerous organizations have formed in recent years to preserve and protect our natural plant heritage.

Map of Northern Rocky Mountains where flowers in this book occur

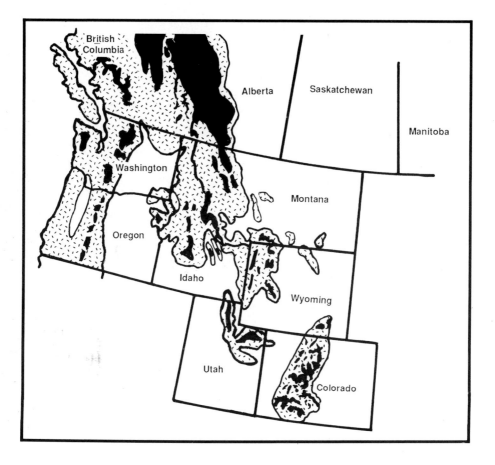

 Alpine & Subalpine

 Forest

Prairie

Lily Family *(Liliaceae)*

GLACIER LILY, Dogtooth Violet

Erythronium grandiflorum Pursh. One or more nodding blossoms spread six brilliant yellow tepals (petals and sepals) that often curve gracefully backward from a smooth green stem, 6 to 12 inches high. Two luxuriant green leaves, smooth, broadly lance shaped and 4 to 6 inches long, emerge from below ground line. The anthers may vary from snowy white to yellow, red, or purple. Glacier lilies sometimes grow in massed abundance in alpine meadows, creating breathtaking natural gardens. Flowers appear soon after snow melt or even push through retreating snow banks. HABITAT: Varies widely from low valleys to moderately dense forests to subalpine or alpine heights. RANGE: Southern British Columbia and Alberta, south to Colorado and Oregon, but mostly on the west slope of the Rockies. COMMENT: We have two varieties of Yellow Glacier Lily. The cream colored "variety" shown in Vol. II, *Forest Wildflowers*, has recently been recognized as a separate species, *E. candidum*. All parts of glacier lily are edible and wild animals, especially bears, feed on them in the spring.

Lily Family *(Liliaceae)*

Lily Family *(Liliaceae)*

SIBERIAN CHIVES

Allium schoenoprasum L. These pretty pink to rose colored onions grow in clumps from clusters of white bulbs and stand 8 to 18 inches tall. Two papery white bracts subtend the globe shaped floral heads, which contain up to 30 individual flowers. Stems are smooth, round, and hollow. Two grasslike leaves, shorter than the flowers, sheath each floral stem at the base. Look for this probable forerunner of cultivated garden chives from late spring to midsummer. HABITAT: Variable, most commonly in damp alpine and subalpine meadows, but also in mid elevation valleys. RANGE: Circumpolar in cold regions, south to Colorado. COMMENT: Wild onions are edible, but indiscriminate digging should be discouraged. Without positive identification, one could mistakenly ingest death camas bulbs with dire results.

ALP LILY

Lloydia serotina (L.) Sweet. A miniature, funnel shaped lily, ½ to ¾ inch in diameter with six white tepals, often tinged with yellowish green and sometimes marked with purple lines. It spreads by underground rhizomes and sprouts from scaly bulbs. The plants stand only 2 to 6 inches high and possess several short grasslike leaves. Blooming occurs usually in July. HABITAT: Alpine tundra, gravelly ridge tops or rocky slopes. RANGE: Most of the high alpine areas of the northern hemisphere, including western North America, the Alps, Himalayas and highest elevations in the British Isles.

Lily Family *(Liliaceae)*　　　　　　　**Lily Family** *(Liliaceae)*

BRONZE BELLS

Stenanthium occidentale Gray. From a small bulb this plant sends up several grasslike leaves and a slender flower stem that may or may not branch in the inflorescence. The flowers resemble small bells with six flaring, sharp pointed tepals and tend to decorate just one side of the stem. They normally hang pendant from pedicels up to 1 inch long and vary in color from greenish yellow to bronze or brownish red. The blossoms appear from mid to late summer. HABITAT: Rocky slopes, meadows or stream banks from sea level on the west coast to timberline in the Rockies. Mostly subalpine. RANGE: Montana to N California and north into Canada. COMMENT: We have just one species in western North America.

FALSE ASPHODEL, Sticky Tofieldia

Tofieldia glutinosa (Michx.) Pers. Pretty creamy or greenish white bunches of small flowers form tight, ball-like heads when first opened, but tend to elongate later in the blooming season. Each blossom displays six tepals and six stamens. The floral stems stand 4 to 20 inches tall. Four to six linear leaves sheath the stems at the base and one or two leafy bracts may arise on the stem. Sticky glands (*glutinosa*) liberally coat the stems, especially near the top. The roots are fibrous, readily distinguishing this species from Death Camas, which rises from an underground bulb. False Asphodel blooms from June into August. HABITAT: Wet calcareous meadows and bogs from low elevations to moist alpine ridges. RANGE: Alaska and N Canada, south to Wyoming, California, and North Carolina.

Lily Family *(Liliaceae)*

BEARGRASS

Xerophyllum tenax (Pursh) Nutt. Tall stately sentinels rise 3 feet or more. A large round or conical plume of small creamy white flowers is supported individually on slender pedicels about 2 inches long. The plants do not bloom every year—perhaps once in seven years or so under a forest canopy, but more frequently on open sites. In a good year Beargrass can be breathtaking. Spreading by thick woody rhizomes, the plants develop dense tussocks of coarse grasslike leaves that have rough edges and are slippery under foot. They may cover entire hillsides or grow sparsely in forested areas. Blooms from June to early August. HABITAT: Fairly dense forest at medium elevation to open alpine slopes. RANGE: British Columbia and Alberta to W Wyoming and California. COMMENT: Beargrass is the official flower of Glacier National Park. Rocky mountain goats eat the tough evergreen leaves in winter and many game animals feed on the succulent flower buds and stems in spring. In the early days Indians wove baskets, clothing, and utensils from the coarse leaves.

Lily Family *(Liliaceae)*   Lily Family *(Liliaceae)*

INDIAN HELLEBORE, Green Cornlily

Veratrum viride Ait. Straight unbranched stalks stand 3 to 5 feet tall. The large green leaves are sessile or possess very short petioles. The largest grow to 1 foot long and 6 inches broad and have 3 to 5 prominent parallel veins between rounded pleats. A mass of small yellowish green flowers crowd the top 6 inches or so of the stem. Several other strands of flowers, 4 to 8 inches long, droop raggedly down on the stem. Blooming occurs in summer. HABITAT-RANGE: Moist meadows and lowlands across Canada, south to North Carolina and Minnesota, but mostly subalpine in the northern Rockies and Cascades. COMMENT: False Hellebore, *V. californicum*, prefers mid elevations in the mountains, as shown in Vol. II, *Forest Wildflowers*. The roots and young shoots of the species are quite poisonous, especially to sheep, but Indians used the plants in various ways as medication.

MOUNTAIN DEATH CAMAS, Alkali Grass

Zigadenus elegans Pursh. Six tepals spread widely, creating a star shaped blossom about ¾ inch across. The points of the star are white or creamy, while a heart shaped gland at the base of each petal makes a greenish yellow, scalloped decoration in the center of each flower. The stems in the inflorescence may or may not branch. Several bright green linear leaves, 4 to 10 inches long, and a single flower stem, usually 1 to 2 feet tall, erupt from a single bulb. Blooming occurs from early to midsummer. HABITAT: Most common in alpine meadows, but may also occur in valleys at medium eleva-tion. RANGE: Alaska south to northern Mexico in the Rockies and in the Washington Cascades. COMMENT: This species is probably not as poisonous as Meadow Death Camas, *Z. venenosus*, shown in Vol. I, *Prairie Wildflowers*, but should be treated with the same respect.

Parsley Family *(Apiaceae, Umbelliferae)*

SANDBERG'S DESERT PARSLEY or BISCUITROOT

Lomatium sandbergii C & R. Although we have half a dozen species of *Lomatium* in our alpine flora, most of them have small localized ranges. Many more species inhabit our prairies and lower mountains, mostly on dry, open sites. Sandberg's Desert Parsley shows bright yellow flowers on the rays of an umbel. The rays are markedly unequal in length. Several stems branch from the base and leaves spring from the base and from the stems. Leaf bases sheath the stems. The leaves divide into many short, linear lobes. Blooming occurs early in the season. HABITAT: Frequents bare ridges and mountain tops. RANGE: Southern Alberta to Montana and Idaho.

Parsley Family *(Apiaceae, Umbelliferae)*   **Parsley Family** *(Apiaceae, Umbelliferae)*

AMERICAN THOROUGHWAX,
Throughwort
Bupleurum americanum C & R. Compound umbels (twice umbellate or umbrella shaped) characterize this unusual inflorescence. The flowers typically display numerous yellow rings with purple centers or they may either be all yellow or purple. Simple linear leaves sprout from the base and on the tuft of stems. This oddly fascinating plant blooms in the summer. HABITAT: Open rocky hillsides or dry gravelly meadows from mid montane to alpine. RANGE: Wyoming and E Idaho to the Yukon. COMMENT: The parsley family is large and diverse, but relatively few species inhabit the alpine zone. See *Oreoxis alpina*, p. 45.

YELLOW MOUNTAIN PARSLEY
Pseudocymopterus montanus (Gray) C & R. This attractive yellow umbel grows in clumps 8 to 20 inches high. The glossy green leaves divide pinnately into widely spaced lobes that further divide irregularly into narrow segments. Pale green leafy wings, striped with dark green veins, decorate the base of the leaf petioles and clasp the stems. Flowering occurs in June and July. HABITAT: Essentially a subalpine dweller of meadows and aspen groves. RANGE: Southern Wyoming to Utah, Texas, and Mexico. COMMENT: Reportedly edible and still used for food by Indians of the Southwest. This species should be tried sparingly or only in an emergency.

ALPINE YARROW

Achillea millefolium var. *alpicola* (Rydb.) Garrett. Several varieties of "ubiquitous yarrow" are generally recognized. A flat inflorescence typifies most varieties, but a small, somewhat rounded inflorescence identifies Alpine Yarrow. Numerous composite heads with three to five small, white, or occasionally pink ray florets, surround a yellowish disc. Bracts with brown or black margins cup the individual floral heads in var. *alpicola*. The feathery, aromatic leaves attach mainly to the stems. Blooms open in late spring and summer. HABITAT: One can find yarrow from the seashore to alpine heights and from open areas to fairly heavy woods, usually on poorer, well drained soils. RANGE: Most of the northern hemisphere. COMMENT: Steeping the leaves makes a flavorful tea, said to have medicinal qualities.

Sunflower Family *(Asteraceae, Compositae)*

Sunflower Family *(Asteraceae, Compositae)*

ORANGE AGOSERIS

Agoseris aurantiaca (Hook.) Greene. Relatively few wildflowers display orange colored blossoms, so recognition of this burnt orange "false dandelion" comes easily. Only strap shaped ray florets occur in the flowers, but the ones in the center of each floral head may resemble disc florets. In seed the fruits bear feathery plumes to help them travel on the wind. The slender leaves grow from the base in a tuft, about half as tall as the flower stems and ordinarily show a few teeth on the margins. The blooms open in summer. HABITAT: Grassy slopes and meadows from high montane to alpine. RANGE: Western United States and across Canada.

16

MOUNTAIN DANDELION, Pale Agoseris

Agoseris glauca (Pursh) Raf. This native perennial looks somewhat like a dandelion, but the strap shaped ray florets are generally wider, less numerous and sharply toothed on the end. The five varieties of Mountain Dandelion vary from 4 inches to 2 feet tall. The leaves may be linear to quite broad and entire to deeply toothed. Milky sap flows from broken stems and leaves. Blooms can appear from midspring through summer. HABITAT: Open areas from low to high elevation. RANGE: Western North America, north of Mexico. COMMENT: We have two other species of yellow flowered *Agoseris*.

Sunflower Family *(Asteraceae, Compositae)*

Sunflower Family *(Asteraceae, Compositae)*

WOOLLY PUSSYTOES

Antennaria lanata (Hook.) Greene. Close to the ground Woolly Pussytoes forms rosettes of narrow leaves that are densely covered with white hairs on both sides. The stems rise 2 to 6 inches high, topped with clusters of 3 to 8 rayless flower heads. Papery bracts, greenish or dirty brown color, surround these heads, which appear in summer. HABITAT: Scattered timber to open rocky ridges from subalpine to alpine vistas. RANGE: Western Canada and south in the mountains to Wyoming and Oregon. COMMENT: Several closely related species resemble this one, including Alpine Pussytoes, *A. alpina*. Some of the other species also form leafy cushions.

17

Sunflower Family *(Asteraceae, Compositae)*   **Sunflower Family** *(Asteraceae, Compositae)*

STICKY ARNICA

Arnica diversifolia Greene. Spreading from underground rhizomes, Sticky Arnica forms clumps of pretty yellow composite flowers. The aerial stems, 6 to 16 inches tall, bear three or four pairs of opposite leaves that vary from heart shaped to narrowly lance shaped with slightly indented to finely toothed margins. The flowers open in late spring and early summer. HABITAT: Rocky slopes and ridges from subalpine to alpine. RANGE: Western mountains from Alberta south to Utah and California. COMMENT: Uncommon in occurrence, Sticky Arnica represents a complex group of hybrids of indeterminate parentage that do not ordinarily produce fertile seeds.

ALPINE SAGE

Artemisia scopulorum Gray. An alpine herb of the sage or sagebrush genus grows in a tuft of mostly basal leaves. Silvery hairs cover the aromatic leaves that are pinnately lobed, the lobes parted again. A few, much reduced stem leaves may also occur and they may be lobed or simple. The stems rise 2 to 12 inches. Several to many floral heads, ½ to ⅜ inch broad, sit tightly on the upper stem. Greenish bracts, prettily lined with black margins, enclose the heads, composed entirely of disc florets. They bloom in mid-summer. HABITAT: Gravelly or rocky alpine heights. RANGE: Southern Montana to New Mexico.

Sunflower Family *(Asteraceae, Compositae)*   **Sunflower Family** *(Asteraceae, Compositae)*

ALPINE ASTER

Aster alpigenus (T. & G.) Gray. Cheerful blue or lavender flowers develop 10 to 40 ray florets. On exposed sites the plants typically grow 2 or 3 inches tall and bear one or two flowers, but may stand 15 inches tall and unfold numerous blossoms in protected locations. The linear leaves attach mostly at the base. Look for Alpine Aster in the summer. HABITAT: Alpine and subalpine. RANGE: Our northern Rocky Mountain area and the cascades and Sierras.

ENGELMANN ASTER

Aster engelmannii (Eat.) Gray. Frequenting the subalpine flora, Engelmann Aster spreads from underground rhizomes and usually stands 2 to 4 feet tall. White to pink or bronzed flowers cluster rather tightly at the top of the stems. The ray florets, about ½ to 1 inch long and not very numerous, often tend to curl in pleasing wreaths. Mostly simple, lance shaped leaves alternate on the stems. It may bloom through the summer. HABITAT: Forest openings to subalpine and alpine reaches. RANGE: Southwestern Canada, south in the mountains to W Washington, Nevada, and Colorado.

Sunflower Family *(Asteraceae, Compositae)*

ALPINE DUSTY MAIDEN

Chaenactis alpina (Gray) Jones. This dwarf version of the more common Hoary Chaenactis, *C. douglasii*, shown in Vol. I, *Prairie Wildflowers,* stands only about 3 inches high. It produces exquisite pinkish floral heads composed entirely of disc florets. The leaves grow mostly in a basal rosette from the root crown and divide into many tiny fernlike segments. Flowering occurs mostly in midsummer. HABITAT: Rocky ridges and talus slopes above timberline. RANGE: The northern Rockies of the contiguous United States.

Sunflower Family *(Asteraceae, Compositae)*

TWEEDY'S THISTLE

Cirsium tweedyi (Rydb.) Petrak. Tweedy's is one of numerous native thistles in the northern Rockies. Some botanists classify it with Elk Thistle, *Cirsium foliosum*. The stems of this latter species do not taper appreciably, whereas the stems of Tweedy's Thistle taper considerably.

The stems of both species are edible when peeled. White woolly hairs and spines cover the pale lavender or creamy flower heads and vicious spines line the margins of deeply lobed leaves. Look for the blooms in summer. HABITAT: Open montane and alpine terrain. RANGE: Canada to Arizona.

DWARF MOUNTAIN FLEABANE, Cutleaf Daisy

Erigeron compositus var. *discoideus* Gray. The leaves of this alpine daisy normally divide once into three lobes. Two other varieties grow at lower elevations and their leaves divide two or three times into 3-lobed segments. Dense hairs sometimes cover the leaves and stems, which stand 2 to 10 inches tall. Solitary flowers about 1 inch across and white, pink, or blue, bloom in summer. HABITAT: Rocky or gravelly ridges and slopes at high elevation. RANGE: Transcontinental in the arctic, south in the Rockies to Arizona. COMMENT: A highly variable species. Rayless forms of this variety occur from Colorado to British Columbia.

Sunflower Family *(Asteraceae, Compositae)*

Sunflower Family *(Asteraceae, Compositae)*

WOOLLY DAISY

Erigeron lanatus Hook. Stylish white or bluish pink daisies, 1 to 1½ inches wide, decorate a low plant 2 or 3 inches high. A solitary flower perches on each floral stem. The plant may or may not branch at the root crown. Dense hairs cover the 1-inch long leaves and stems. Look for them to bloom in summer. HABITAT: Rocky alpine ridges and crevices. RANGE: Colorado north to the Canadian Rockies. COMMENT: Rydberg's Daisy, a similar white to violet alpine species, has only a few hairs on the leaves. Woolly Daisy appears on Montana's rare species list.

Sunflower Family *(Asteraceae, Compositae)*   **Sunflower Family** *(Asteraceae, Compositae)*

BLACKHEADED DAISY

Erigeron melanocephalus Nels. These small white daisies grow in colonies from spreading rhizomes. Long woolly hairs, colored dark purple to almost black, coat the involucre, the underside of the flower head. Most of the leaves sprout from the plant base, but a few small leaves cling to the short, 2 to 6 inch, stems. Each stem supports a single flower head that blooms in mid- to late summer. HABITAT: Subalpine and alpine meadows and slopes, where moist but well drained and often near snow banks. RANGE: Wyoming to New Mexico.

ALPINE DAISY, Oneflowered Daisy

Erigeron simplex Greene. This charming alpine daisy, about 1½ inches in diameter, displays 50 or more pink, lavender or rarely white ray florets. One or a few stems rise from a perennial root crown, each stem topped by a solitary flower. Most of the simple leaves sprout from the root crown, but a few smaller leaves attach to the flower stem. Long woolly white hairs coat the stems and base of the flower heads. It blooms in midsummer. HABITAT: Various alpine situations. RANGE: The Rocky Mountains of the contiguous states.

Sunflower Family *(Asteraceae, Compositae)*

LYALL'S GOLDENWEED

Haplopappus lyallii Gray. Numerous woody branches sprout from the base of this semishrub. It also spreads from underground rhizomes and commonly forms dense clumps. Solitary flowers perch on leafy stems, 1 to 4 inches high, blooming in mid- to late summer. HABITAT: Gravelly or rocky alpine areas. RANGE: Colorado to Nevada and north to the Canadian Rockies.

Sunflower Family *(Asteraceae, Compositae)*

ALPINE HULSEA, Alpine Gold

Hulsea algida Gray. Bright yellow sunflowers, 2 to 3½ inches across, often grow in patches. Several stems sprout from a taproot crown, each one bearing a single flower. Long woolly white hairs clothe the underside of the flower heads and short sticky hairs cover the 4 to 10 inch stems and leaves. Basal leaves to 6 inches long have scalloped edges and are quite succulent. Blooms from mid- to late summer. HABITAT: Rock crevices and talus slopes at alpine heights. RANGE: Montana and N Wyoming to N Nevada and E California.

Sunflower Family *(Asteraceae, Compositae)*

OLD MAN OF THE MOUNTAINS,
Alpine Sunflower

Hymenoxys grandiflora (T. & G.) Parker. This hardy high mountain native may send up one or several blossoms, 2 to 4 inches in diameter, on short stems that sprout directly from a taproot crown. The showy ray florets display 3-lobed tips. Long soft hairs densely cover the stems, flower bracts, and the leaves, which have several deeply divided linear lobes. The plants bloom from June to August. HABITAT: Exposed rocky or gravelly alpine slopes. RANGE: Utah and Colorado to Idaho and S Montana. COMMENT: The flowers, appearing much too large for the rest of the plant, always face the rising sun.

Sunflower Family *(Asteraceae, Compositae)*

ALPINE SAWWORT

Saussurea weberi Hulten. Unusual and very uncommon, relatively large flower heads of Alpine Sawwort sit on rather stubby stems, which are closely beset with shining, alternate, lance-shaped leaves. The singular flower heads display slender, dark purple to nearly black stamens and styles that protrude markedly but rather haphazardly from dense tufts of capillary or slightly plumy bristles. Blooms generally appear in midsummer. HABITAT: Rocky alpine vistas. RANGE: Montana to Colorado along the mountain crest. COMMENT: A more northerly species, *S. densa*, reaches our region in NW Montana.

Sunflower Family *(Asteraceae, Compositae)*

ALPINE TOWNSENDIA

Townsendia montana Jones. An exquisite little composite, blue or violet or occasionally pink or white, grows in a tuft of spatula-shaped leaves. The leaves may be smooth or dotted with short stiff hairs. As with most Townsendias the flowers dwarf the rest of the plant. They open in July and August. HABITAT: Rocky slopes and ridges, subalpine and alpine. RANGE: Western Montana to W Colorado, NE Oregon and Utah. COMMENT: A larger and perhaps more common species, *T. parryi* occurs in most of our region. Both species can easily be mistaken for asters or daisies.

Borage Family *(Boraginaceae)*

ALPINE FORGET-ME-NOT

Eritrichium aretioides (Chamisso) de Candolle. *Eritrichium nanum* (Vill.) Schrad. Five petals, fused at the base in a short tube, flare widely into round, open-faced (rotate) flowers about ¼ inch in diameter or less. They dot or sometimes literally cover this low matted plant. The blossoms vary from occasional, white mutants or pale to deep blue. They usually display yellow or white center accents. The small hairy leaves form a dense cushion normally only 1 to 3 inches thick, which adapts the plant ideally to withstand harsh winds and blowing ice crystals in its alpine-arctic home. Blooms open early in the alpine growing season. HABITAT: Common on exposed rocky or gravelly ridges and slopes from high subalpine prairies to mountain tops. RANGE: Circumpolar in arctic regions, south to New Mexico. COMMENTS: We have two species of alpine *Eritrichium: E. aretioides* sports greenish grey leaves with soft wavy hairs, while silvery leaves covered by short straight hairs identify *E. howardii.* Alpine Forget-Me-Not richly rewards the alpine visitor who will seek out these dazzling blooms. See the back cover.

Borage Family *(Boraginaceae)*

Borage Family *(Boraginaceae)*

ALPINE BLUEBELL

Mertensia alpina (Torr.) Don. Numerous dainty, bell shaped blossoms, less than ½ inch long, crowd the ends of several stems, 2 to 10 inches high. The floral tube and bell are approximately the same length in this species. One can easily distinguish Alpine Bluebell from other *Mertensias*, because the anthers remain wholly enclosed within the tube and are thus not visible in the flower's throat to the casual glance. The flowers generally emerge in midsummer. HABITAT: Well drained meadows to rock crevices at alpine and subalpine altitudes. RANGE: Idaho and Montana to New Mexico. COMMENT: Greenleaf Mertensia, *M. viridis*, appears quite similar, but the anthers peek out of the tube in that species.

WOOD FORGET-ME-NOT, Alpine Forget-Me-Not

Myosotis sylvatica var. *alpestris* (Schmidt) Koch. *Myosotis alpestris* Schmidt. This lovely forget-me-not, the state flower of Alaska, grows in an upright spray of stems, 4 to 10 inches high. The stems may or may not branch. Yellow, red, or white center eyes, sometimes all on the same plant, contrast brilliantly with five deep blue petals. Long soft hairs clothe the oblong leaves that erupt in a tuft from the base and some smaller sessile leaves grace the flower stems. Blooms appear from late spring into summer. HABITAT: Meadows and grassy slopes from subalpine upward. RANGE: Circumboreal. In North America, Alaska to Colorado and Utah. COMMENT: At least four genera of borages: *Cryptantha, Eritrichium, Hackelia* and *Myosotis*, are called forget-me-not.

Borage Family *(Boraginaceae)*

SMALL BLUEBELL, Long Flowered Bluebell

Mertensia longiflora Greene. A low, delicate bluebell, 2 to 8 inches tall, the flowers grow in a tight cluster and seem much too long for the rest of the plant. The floral tube in this species is 2 or 3 times as long as the bell. Oval leaves clasp the upper stem, while petioles sometimes support a few lower leaves, if present. This one blooms very early in the season. HABITAT: Sagebrush prairies east of the Cascades to subalpine ridges in the Rockies. RANGE: Southern Canadian Rockies to Montana, Idaho, and N California. COMMENT: Small Bluebell could be mistaken for Leafy Bluebell, *M. oblongifolia*, but the latter has numerous petioled leaves that are long, pointed, and quite slender.

ALPINE WALLFLOWER, Snowy
Erysimum

Erysimum nivale (Greene) Rydb. From a tight clump of narrow leaves, 1½ to 2½ inches long and rough to the touch due to short stiff hairs, rise one to several flower stems, 2 to 10 inches high. Tight clusters of blooms generally begin to appear when the stems are very short and continue to open as the stems elongate. Each blossom has four petals in the shape of a cross, typical of the family, cheerful yellow or sometimes purple at very high altitudes. Blooming begins quite early in the alpine season—June to July. HABITAT: Open alpine slopes and ridges. RANGE: The central Rockies: S Wyoming, Colorado, and E Utah. COMMENT: We have several species of wallflower, but the others mostly prefer lower elevations.

Mustard Family *(Brassicaceae, Cruciferae)*

Mustard Family *(Brassicaceae, Cruciferae)*

COMB DRABA or PAYSON'S DRABA

Draba oligosperma Hook., OR *Draba paysonii* Macb. A low cushion plant often densely covered with sparkling yellow, 4-petaled, cross-shaped flowers. The flower stems, ½ to 3 inches high, bear no leaves and carry one or a few blossoms in a raceme. Microscopic hairs that branch pinnately, like two combs back-to-back, cover the short, closely-packed, narrow leaves of Comb Draba. Forked hairs identify Payson's Draba, among several low tufted species. They bloom early in the season to midsummer. HABITAT: High open prairies and foothills to alpine ridges. RANGE: Western United States and Canada.

SIBERIAN SMELOWSKIA

Smelowskia calycina (Steph.) Mey. These plants usually grow in a dense cushion or tuft, branching from a taproot crown. The flowers have four white petals that occasionally display a pink or purple tinge. Flower stems stand 2 to 8 inches, topped by a crowded cluster of blossoms. Most of the leaves, quite hairy and deeply lobed pinnately, grow from the base of the plant. Look for the blooms from June to August. HABITAT: Rocky talus slopes or outcrops near or above timberline. RANGE: Eastern Siberia and W North America, south to Colorado and Utah.

Mustard Family *(Brassicaceae, Cruciferae)*

Mustard Family *(Brassicaceae, Cruciferae)*

MOUNTAIN CANDYTUFT, Wild Candytuft

Thlaspi montanum L. Clusters of small white, 4-petaled flowers decorate the top of tufted, unbranching stems, 2 to 10 inches tall. A rosette of oval leaves, commonly wavy on the margins, surrounds the base of the stems and tiny clasping leaves, shaped like arrow heads, alternate on the stems. Blooming occurs from May to August. HABITAT: Open sites from mid elevations to alpine. RANGE: Western North America and Europe. COMMENT: Field Pennycress, *T. arvense*, is a very common introduced weed of cultivated fields and road sides.

PARRY'S HAREBELL or BLUEBELL

Campanula parryi Gray. This pretty little harebell, normally solitary and upright on slender stems, 4 to 12 inches tall, spreads widely from underground roots. Five pale to deep blue petals fuse together at the base forming a shallow bell. The leaves, oval below, become narrowed upward and possess fringes of hairs along the lower edges. A mid-summer bloomer. HABITAT: Gravelly scree slopes and meadows at subalpine and higher elevations. RANGE: Washington Cascades to W Montana and south through the Rockies. COMMENT: We have two varieties: *idahoensis* in the north and a larger variety, *parryi*, southward. Arctic Harebell, *C. uniflora*, could easily be mistaken for this one.

Harebell Family *(Campanulaceae)*

Harebell Family *(Campanulaceae)*

COMMON HAREBELL

Campanula rotundifolia L. Common and widespread, this perennial varies considerably in its growth habit. While linear stem leaves predominate, the basal leaves on some plants are quite round, as the species name implies. On others only linear leaves occur or the round ones wither early. Plants in the lowlands may grow 6 to 20 inches tall and bear numerous blue to somewhat lavender, bell shaped and nodding flowers. The dwarfed, 2 to 3 inch tall alpine specimens pictured here each support just one full sized or oversized blossom. It blooms from late spring to the end of the season. HABITAT: Variable from low elevation to alpine, usually on dry, open sites. RANGE: Hemispheric, south of arctic regions.

Harebell Family *(Campanulaceae)*

ROUGH HAREBELL or BELLFLOWER

Campanula scabrella Engelm. Groups of small showy bluebells spring from a branching taproot crown. Rough Harebell closely resembles the famous Piper's Bellflower of Olympic National Park. Rough Harebell's leaves are smooth on the edges, while Piper's Bellflower has sharp teeth on the margins. This one blooms in summer. HABITAT: Rocky alpine slopes. RANGE: The northern Rockies in our area and the Cascades.

ARCTIC SANDWORT

Arenaria obtusiloba (Rydb.) Fern. Many woody stems spread along the ground and over small rocks from a central root, forming loose or dense cushions up to 3 feet in diameter. Short linear leaves persist on the stems for several years adding denseness to the mat. The flowers, about ¼ inch across, have five white rounded petals with greenish-yellow tinting or striping at the base. It blooms through the summer. HABITAT: Rocky or gravelly meadows and slopes from the arctic south to subalpine and alpine areas in the mountains. RANGE: Alaska to Oregon and New Mexico and in Labrador and Greenland. COMMENT: More than a dozen species of *Arenaria* inhabit the Rockies. They seem to prefer sandy growing sites and can be difficult to distinguish, one from the other.

Pink Family *(Caryophyllaceae)*

Pink Family *(Caryophyllaceae)*

ROSS' SANDWORT

Arenaria rossii var. *apetala* Maguire. This unusual alpine plant forms dense cushions of linear leaves, ⅛ to ¼ inch long, triangular in cross section and obtusely pointed. Tiny five-pointed stars, yellowish-green in color, composed only of sepals, rise above the cushion to attract one's attention. It "blooms" in midsummer. HABITAT: Gravelly or rocky alpine ridges and slopes. RANGE: Alberta to Wyoming and Idaho. COMMENT: The type variety, *rossii*, occurs more commonly and displays white, rounded petals.

34

ROCKY MOUNTAIN NAILWORT, Alpine Whitlowwort

Paronychia pulvinata Gray. A very low, matted perennial herb produces tiny, greenish-yellow flowers that have no floral stems. They nestle among equally small, rounded leaves, only about ¼ inch long, that also grow sessile on short prostrate stems. White papery stipules (bracts) subtend the tightly crowded leaves. Blooming occurs in late spring and early summer. HABITAT: Dry gravelly or rocky ridges and slopes, mostly above 10,000 feet elevation. RANGE: The central Rockies, Wyoming, Utah, Colorado, and southward. COMMENTS: Several other species at lower elevations possess spine-tipped leaves. The common names refer to early day uses of these plants to treat infected finger- and toenails.

Pink Family *(Caryophyllaceae)*

Pink Family *(Caryophyllaceae)*

ALPINE LANTERNS

Lychnis apetala L. Ten prominent purple stripes decorate an inflated calyx, pinched at the throat to resemble a miniature oriental lantern. The amusing little flowers grow in clumps of linear basal leaves. Each stem usually bears a single blossom that nods at the peak of blooming. Pink or purplish petals mostly or entirely hide within the calyx. Short straight hairs, tipped with sticky glands, densely clothe the stems and calyces. It is rare or uncommon at best and blooms in July and August. HABITAT: High alpine sites. RANGE: From the Arctic south to Colorado.

35

Pink Family *(Caryophyllaceae)*

MOSS CAMPION, Moss Pink

Silene acaulis L. One of the more common and best known alpine inhabitants, this mat-forming perennial radiates short woody branches along the ground. Many crowded stems rise about 1 inch and bear short linear leaves. The leaves commonly remain on the stems for several years, adding to the cushion effect of the plant. Gorgeous pink to deep rose or occasionally white flowers bloom on the stem ends, often blanketing the mats, to the delight of alpine explorers. HABITAT: Rocky ridges and slopes. RANGE: Circumpolar in arctic regions and south in high mountains to Arizona and New Hampshire. COMMENT: Moss Campion, always exposed in nature to the most severe weather conditions, adapts quite readily to rock gardens.

Stonecrop Family *(Crassulaceae)*

Stonecrop Family *(Crassulaceae)*

ROSE CROWN, Queen's Crown, Red Orpine

Sedum rhodanthum Gray. These lovely pink and white flowers each show five sharp pointed petals. They crowd closely together and display accents of dark red or purple stamens. The plants normally send up several stems from the base, 3 to 12 inches tall, covered with many short, smooth, succulent leaves. Look for them to flower in mid-summer. HABITAT: Wet meadows and stream banks in subalpine and alpine regions. RANGE: The Rocky Mountains south of Canada.

KING'S CROWN, Roseroot

Sedum roseum (L.) Scop. King's Crown generally stands shorter than Rose Crown, usually not exceeding 6 inches in height. Tiny 4-petaled, blood red to dark maroon flowers press tightly together in terminal heads and turn nearly black with age. The succulent leaves may have smooth, entire margins or show some scallops, as well as reddish-colored borders. It blooms from late spring to midsummer. HABITAT: Rocky or well drained alpine areas, where moist early in the season. RANGE: Circumpolar in the far north and south in the mountains to Colorado, California, Pennsylvania, and Maine.

SWAMP LAUREL, Alpine Laurel, Bog Wintergreen

Kalmia microphylla (Hook.) Heller. This low prostrate shrub spreads by underground stems or by layering and normally stands less than 8 inches high. The stems branch sparingly, each branch end bearing 3 to 10 or more stunning pink flowers. Five petals that curl backward at the tip, cohere at the base to effect a shallow cup about ½ inch across. Ten prominent stamens appear dark red to almost black. The anthers rest in little pockets in the petals until an insect disturbs them, when they snap upright to sprinkle the intruder with pollen and ensure cross-pollination. Narrow leaves have smooth green surfaces above and grey hairy ones below. The leaf edges curl under. Blooms open early but may continue through the summer. HABITAT: Lake shores and other wet places in high mountains. RANGE: Western North America, south in the Rockies to Colorado. COMMENT: A taller species, *polifolia*, ranges at lower elevation along both coasts and across Canada.

Heath Family *(Ericaceae)*

Heath Family *(Ericaceae)*

WHITE MOUNTAIN HEATHER

Cassiope mertensiana (Bong.) Don. Masses of miniature white bells nod a greeting to alpine visitors, the bells often supported by bright red stems and sepals. Five short rounded petals curl backward on the lip of each bell. From the base shrubby branches spread along the ground, sometimes covering large patches. The stems rise from the branches, 2 to 10 inches high. Four rows of short overlapping, scale-like leaves clothe the stems. Blooms occur in July and August. HABITAT: Slopes with fairly deep soil near or above timberline. RANGE: Montana to NE Oregon and California and north into Canada.

PINK MOUNTAIN HEATH, Red Heather

Phyllodoce empetriformis (Sw.) Don. This low shrub branches profusely and frequently creates a dense ground cover, 4 to 12 inches thick. The small, bell shaped flowers, intense pink to rose, cluster on branch ends and nod gracefully on slender, reddish-hairy pedicels. Pistils protrude from the bells but not the stamens. The flowers resemble White Mountain Heather, but the color and the leaves differentiate the two. Needle-like, evergreen leaves densely cover the branches, reminding one of fir boughs. This exquisite floral display occurs in July and August. HABITAT: Moist alpine meadows and slopes. RANGE: Wyoming to California and north to Alaska and the Yukon.

Heath Family *(Ericaceae)*

Heath Family *(Ericaceae)*

LABRADOR TEA, Trapper's Tea

Ledum glandulosum Nutt. Several to many charming white flowers crowd the branch tips of a low, rambling shrub. Each flower has about 10 prominently protruding stamens. The oval leaves possess a leathery texture above, white hairs beneath and edges that usually roll under. Blooming occurs in midsummer. HABITAT: Moist woods and stream banks at medium to subalpine situations in the mountains. RANGE: Canadian Rockies south to Wyoming, NE Oregon and the Washington Cascades. COMMENT: Early explorers brewed tea from the leaves of a similar species, *L. groenlandicum*, with reddish hairs under the leaves.

39

Heath Family *(Ericaceae)*

Heath Family *(Ericaceae)*

YELLOW MOUNTAIN HEATH (Heather)
Phyllodoce glanduliflora (Hook.) Coville.
A low spreading shrub similar in growth
habit to Pink Mountain Heath except for
the flowers, which are urn shaped
(pinched at the throat) and yellow or
greenish-yellow. Many sticky glandular
hairs coat the exterior of both flowers
and stems. They bloom in July and
early August. HABITAT: Moist sites in
alpine country. RANGE: Coincides with
Pink Mountain Heath. COMMENT: Pink
and yellow species sometimes hybridize, but only near both parents.

WHITE RHODODENDRON
Rhododendron albiflorum Hook. Brown
or purplish spots normally embellish
the petals of these creamy white, ¾ to
1 inch wide flowers. They originate in
the axils of leaves of the previous
year's growth. These shrubs stand 2 to
6 feet tall. The flowers open in late
spring or early summer. HABITAT:
Stream banks, lake shores and other
wet places in high elevation woods or
subalpine zones. RANGE: Colorado,
Oregon, and W Montana and north into
Canada. COMMENT: The only
rhododendron in the Rockies, it lacks
the spectacular, colorful blooms of its
close relative, *R. macrophyllum*, the
state flower of Washington.

Pea Family *(Fabaceae, Leguminosae)* | Pea Family *(Fabaceae, Leguminosae)*

ALPINE MILKVETCH, Mountain Locoweed

Astragalus alpinus L. This admirable little pea has ten or more flowers closely spaced on a stem bare of leaves and attached with short pedicels—a raceme. The flowers, ¼ to ½ inch long possess lavender or bluish banner and keel petals and white or yellowish wing petals. The darkest coloration usually marks the tip of the keel petal. Thirteen or more oval leaflets, about the same length as the flowers and pinnately compound, comprise a leaf. The plants spread widely from strong underground roots, ordinarily forming loose ground cover. Blossoms may open quite early and last into midsummer. HABITAT: Moist sites in subalpine and alpine areas. RANGE: Arctic regions of the world, south in our mountains to New Mexico. COMMENT: A dense coating of black hairs covers the small drooping pods of this species.

THISTLE MILKVETCH, Matvetch

Astragalus kentrophyta var. *implexus* (Canby) Barneby. A low mat-forming plant only 2 or 3 inches high. Each leaf has 5 to 9 small narrow leaflets that taper to short sharp spines at the tip. Numerous purple pea blossoms nestle among the leaves, which are usually greyish-green from a coating of short straight hairs. Blooming can occur through the summer. HABITAT: High sagebrush prairie to wooded subalpine and open alpine slopes. RANGE: Southern Alberta to Nevada and New Mexico. COMMENT: More than a dozen species of *Astragalus* inhabit our alpine regions.

WESTERN SWEETVETCH

Hedysarum occidentale Greene. A raceme of pink to dark magenta blossoms adorn the upper end of upright stems and droop, at least in the lower portion of the inflorescence. Keel petals are generally longer than banners and wings. Leaves start from nodes along the stem and have 9 to 21 oval leaflets, ½ to 1 inch long. The blooms can persist from June into September. HABITAT: Open woods and grassy slopes above and below treeline. RANGE: Idaho, Montana, Wyoming, and Colorado. COMMENT: We have two other similarly colored species: *H. alpinum*, a smaller plant of high mountains and *H. boreale*, which prefers prairies and lower mountain habitats.

Pea Family *(Fabaceae, Leguminosae)*

Pea Family *(Fabaceae, Leguminosae)*

WHITE SWEETVETCH, Yellow Hedysarum

Hedysarum sulphurescens Rydb. This white or pale yellow *Hedysarum* grows in clumps 1 to 2 feet tall in the montane forest zone, but much smaller at high elevations. In the open forest it usually exhibits more than 20 blossoms per stem, but fewer in alpine habitat. The leaves, which arise on the floral stems, each possess about 13 oval leaflets. They bloom from June to August. HABITAT: Forest openings and scattered timber to alpine. RANGE: Wyoming to Alberta and west to Washington and British Columbia.

SILVERY LUPINE

Lupinus argenteus Pursh. Several stems that may or may not branch rise from a woody root crown, 6 to 16 inches high. The leaves grow on the stems, are palmately compound, usually with 6 to 9 narrow leaflets that are silky hairy on the underside. The deep blue to white flowers display white or reddish centers on the banner petals. They create pretty racemes at the upper end of the stems. Blooms appear in late spring and early summer. HABITAT: Low elevation prairies to open forests to alpine. RANGE: Western mountains east of the Cascades. COMMENT: The lupines hybridize extensively and are often difficult to identify. Silvery Lupine is so variable that nearly 50 different scientific names have been assigned to it by various authors. A fairly distinct variety, *depressus*, occurs in alpine areas from central Idaho and Montana southward.

Pea Family *(Fabaceae, Leguminosae)*

Pea Family *(Fabaceae, Leguminosae)*

CUSICK'S CRAZYWEED

Oxytropis campestris var. *cusickii* (Greene) Barneby. These dwarf legumes unfold crowded racemes of five to ten flowers, pale yellow to off-white. The showy upright banner petals reflex sharply (bend backward). Eleven to 17 lance shaped leaflets form a leaf.

Blooming occurs in June and July. HABITAT: High montane to open alpine slopes. RANGE: Alberta to Colorado and Utah. COMMENT: This species has three varieties. The other two are larger plants that normally grow at lower altitudes. They can easily be mistaken for Silky Crazyweed, *O. sericea*.

HAYDEN'S ALPINE CLOVER

Trifolium haydenii Porter. This sprawling plant sometimes forms mats, but more commonly grows in loose patches. Floral stems 2 inches long support heads of five to twenty flowers that vary from cream to bright rose. A leaf consists of three broad leaflets to ¾ inch long with small teeth on the margins. Look for this delicate beauty in July and early August. HABITAT: Meadows and scattered forest at high mountain and subalpine altitudes; infrequent above timberline. RANGE: Endemic to the Beartooth-Yellowstone Park region of S Montana and NW Wyoming.

Pea Family *(Fabaceae, Leguminosae)*

Pea Family *(Fabaceae, Leguminosae)*

WHIPROOT CLOVER

Trifolium dasyphyllum T. & G. White or yellowish banner petals, often tipped with dark red or purple, provide gorgeous backgrounds for the rose to purple wing and keel petals. These distinctive floral heads rise 1 to 3 inches, composed of up to 30 individual flowers, tightly clustered. The plants are tufted or spreading and somewhat mat forming. It flowers from mid- to late summer. HABITAT: Rocky slopes and ridges, subalpine to alpine. RANGE: Southern Montana to Utah and southward. COMMENT: Several species of alpine clover grace the high regions of the central Rockies and grow nowhere else.

44

Pea Family *(Fabaceae, Leguminosae)*   **Pea Family** *(Fabaceae, Leguminosae)*

DWARF CLOVER, Deer Clover

Trifolium nanum Torr. Tiny three-leaf clovers, the leaflets about ¼ inch long, form low dense mats. One to three relatively large flowers top each flower stem, an unusual inflorescence for a clover. These enchanting blossoms display bright red or pink parallel stripes on a white or light-colored base. They bloom in July and August and darken to brown or purple in age. HABITAT: Alpine ridges and rocky slopes, ordinarily above 10,000 feet elevation. RANGE: Southern Montana to Utah and New Mexico. COMMENT: Alpine Parsley, *Oreoxis alpina*, the yellow umbel in the foreground, commonly occurs in the central and southern Rockies on gravelly and rocky perches above timberline.

PARRY'S CLOVER, Alpine Clover

Trifolium parryi Gray. These plants ordinarily grow in a tuft from a taproot crown. The flowers create dense heads of 10 to 30 blossoms, deep pink to rose and quite fragrant. Papery bracts subtend the lovely flower heads. All of the leaves sprout from the base, the leaflets about 1 inch long and sharply toothed. Numerous stems, 1 to 2 inches tall, support the floral heads just above to well above the leaves. The flowers open in mid- to late summer. HABITAT: Alpine and subalpine slopes where rocky or gravelly. RANGE: Southern Idaho and Montana to New Mexico.

Bleeding Heart Family *(Fumariaceae)*

Gentian Family *(Gentianaceae)*

STEER'S HEAD

Dicentra uniflora Kell. Perhaps the most improbable flower in the Rockies, Steer's Head unmistakably resembles the head of a cow with large horns. It blooms very early, is small and hugs the ground. Two petals fuse at the base and enclose the stamens and pistil in a sac and look like a cow's face. Two other petals resemble an animal's horns. Both flowers and leaves sprout from the root crown deep underground and emerge separately. The leaves divide into 3 or 5 main lobes and they divide again irregularly. HABITAT: Sagebrush plains to open subalpine ridges. RANGE: Western Montana and Wyoming to Utah, California, and Washington.

MONUMENT PLANT, Green Gentian

Frasera speciosa Dougl. Numerous leaves, smooth and oblong or lance shaped and 10 to 20 inches long, grow in a tuft. The plant lives without blooming for perhaps 20 to 60 years, storing energy in a strong taproot system. Finally the plant sends up one central, unbranched stem, 2 to 5 feet tall, bearing whorls of stem leaves that gradually reduce upwards. These stately, conical plants bloom once and then die.

Numerous flowers erupt from the axils of the upper leaf whorls. From a distance the flowers appear quite plain, but on close inspection they are stunning. Purple flecks dot the four greenish white, open-faced petals. Pinkish hairs fringe two oval or linear nectary glands near the base of each petal. Four gracefully curving stamens and a deeply divided, hair-like corona surround a prominent green ovary at the center of the blossom. Blooming occurs in June and July. The dried stalks may remain standing for several years. HABITAT: High prairies to subalpine and alpine meadows and slopes. RANGE: Both sides of the Rockies from Washington and Montana to N Mexico.

MONUMENT PLANT, Green Gentian

PARRY'S GENTIAN, Rocky Mountain Pleated Gentian

Gentiana parryi Engelm. The blossoms of Parry's Gentian closely resemble Explorer's Gentian, but four or five flowers normally crowd the top of a single stem. The pleats between the petals usually end in just one sharp tooth or filament. The blooms stay closed on cloudy days, perhaps to keep the upright flowers from collecting rain water. Several pairs of broad, bract-like leaves subtend the flowers. The lower leaves are lance shaped and sessile. Blooms open in late summer. HABITAT: High mountain meadows and stream banks. RANGE: Southern Montana and south in the Rockies. COMMENT: This alpine specimen represents a confusing, complex group of closely related species or varieties that occur in a wide diversity of habitats.

Gentian Family *(Gentianaceae)*

Gentian Family *(Gentianaceae)*

ARCTIC GENTIAN

Gentiana algida Pall. Five petals, fused together and pleated between the petal lobes for most of their length, compose a deep floral cup. Pretty purple specks or splotches decorate the petals both inside and out. Several of these white or cream colored tubular flowers, 1½ to 2 inches long, crowd the top of short upright stems. The plant may send up one or more stems from a perennial base. Blooming occurs late in the season, mostly in August. HABITAT: High altitude tundra and meadows, commonly from 10,000 feet elevation and upward in our area. RANGE: New Mexico to the arctic and in Siberia.

Gentian Family *(Gentianaceae)*

EXPLORER'S GENTIAN, Bog Gentian

Gentiana calycosa Griseb. Dazzling dark blue to purple (rarely yellowish) bells, speckled greenish-yellow inside and often fading to green or pale yellow at the base, stand upright about 1½ inches long. The flowers display five rounded petal lobes with pleats between the lobes. Each pleat usually ends in two fine, sharp-pointed teeth between the petals. Several stems, 2 to 10 inches tall, grow in a tuft from a fleshy root. Solitary flowers, or occasionally as many as three, terminate the stems. Smooth opposite leaves sprout from the stems. The basal pair of leaves fuse together enclosing the stem, while the upper leaves are oval or heart shaped and sessile. Look for these elegant blooms from mid- to late summer. HABITAT: Wet alpine or subalpine bogs, meadows, or slopes on fairly deep soil. RANGE: Widespread in the high mountains of North America.

WESTERN FRINGED GENTIAN,
Feather Gentian

Gentiana thermalis Kuntze *Gentiana detonsa* Rottb. These elegant blue or bluish purple flowers, 1½ to 3 inches long, flare at the throat into four raggedly fringed petals from floral tubes that commonly twist as they close. They may show dark purple parallel stripes. The flower base sits in a green or yellowish calyx tube, topped by four to seven sharply pointed lobes. Fringed Gentian is an annual with two to four pairs of opposite leaves. The stems grow 4 to 16 inches tall and may branch several times near the base. Blooms open only in full sunshine in mid- to late summer. HABITAT: Stream banks and moist meadows from medium elevation to lower alpine. RANGE: Circumpolar. Across Canada to Alaska and south in the Rockies to Mexico. COMMENT: Abundant in Yellowstone National Park where it is the official park flower. The species name, *thermalis*, indicates the plant's occurrence near Yellowstone's thermal features.

Gentian Family *(Gentianaceae)*

Gentian Family *(Gentianaceae)*

MOSS GENTIAN

Gentiana prostrata Haenke. A tiny gentian likes to nestle in the moss or grass of high alpine tundra. Four or five petals, pleated in a short tube, flare widely at the throat into a star shape. Bright yellow stamens are visible, deeply seated in the floral tube. A passing cloud or other shade will cause the flowers to close quickly. Moss-like leaves clothe the stem, ½ to 6 inches high. Blooms open in midsummer. HABITAT: Meadows, bogs, and grassy ridges in high alpine country. RANGE: Circumboreal, south to Colorado, Utah, and N California; also found in the Andes of South America.

50

Gentian Family *(Gentianaceae)*

Gentian Family *(Gentianaceae)*

NORTHERN GENTIAN

Gentianella amarella (L.) Börner. Our alpine flora includes very few annual wildflowers. Northern Gentian is an annual or biennial that does find a niche at high elevations, but not exclusively there. The plants stand 2 to 16 inches high, often branching several times and bearing leaves at the base and on the stems. Narrow upright trumpets spring from upper leaf axils and display a beautiful feathery fringe in the throat of each tube. Colors of the pointed petals may vary from pale blue, lavender, or violet to yellowish or even white. One might find the blooms throughout the summer. HABITAT: Meadows and other damp places from seashore to alpine. RANGE: Most of the northern hemisphere from medium to high latitudes.

BOG SWERTIA, Star Gentian, Star Felwort

Swertia perennis L. Pale blue, purplish or greenish-blue petals with intricately striped patterns on five-pointed stars announce Bog Swertia. Close inspection reveals two small, round pits near the base of each petal, surrounded by colorful hairs. The stems rise 6 to 12 inches from spreading underground rhizomes and usually occur in uncrowded patches. Smooth leaves, oblong or oval, mostly spring from the base, but one to three pair of small opposite leaves cling to the stem. These delightful flowers open in August. HABITAT: High mountain marshes, mossy banks and alpine meadows. RANGE: The mountains of western North America, Europe, and Asia.

Gooseberry Family *(Grossulariaceae)*

SWAMP GOOSEBERRY, Black Currant, Prickly Currant

Ribes lacustre (Pers.) Poir. This spreading shrub is armed with three to seven sharp thorns at each node and many smaller prickles on younger stems between the nodes. One to two inch maple-like leaves may bear some hairs but not sticky glandular ones. Several ornate little flowers about ¼ inch across, saucer shaped and yellowish-green to bright red, form short racemes in leaf axils. The rounded sepals are fused at the base and support a flat disc in the center of the flower. Five shorter petals attach to the edge of the disc. Bitter, dark purple berries, liberally covered with sticky glandular hairs, develop in late summer. HABITAT: Moist woods and stream banks to rocky subalpine and lower alpine ridges. RANGE: Alaska, most of Canada and south to Pennsylvania, Colorado and California. COMMENT: One may easily mistake Swamp Gooseberry for Alpine Prickly Currant, *R. montigenum*, which has sticky hairs on the leaves and reddish berries. *R. coloradense* also bears similar flowers but no spines.

Waterleaf Family *(Hydrophyllaceae)*

SILKY PHACELIA, Purple Fringe

Phacelia sericea (Grah.) Gray. A lovely dense spike, often elongated, of glorious deep blue to purple flowers. Many purple stamens radiate outwards tipped with yellow anthers, making the inflorescence fairly bristle. The plants send up several stems, usually not over 1 foot high, that grow in a clump from a branching taproot crown. Long silky hairs coat the leaves, which have irregular pinnate lobes and long petioles at the base, but grow nearly sessile and smaller up the stem. It blooms early in the season and into summer. HABITAT: Rocky or gravelly meadows and dry slopes in subalpine and alpine terrain. RANGE: New Mexico to N California and north into Canada. COMMENT: We have about a dozen species of *Phacelia* in the northern Rockies, three of them alpine residents.

MOUNTAIN MONARDELLA, False Horsemint, Coyote Mint

Monardella odoratissima Benth. A dense spreading clump of unbranched stems stand 6 to 18 inches high. Each stem bears a flat-topped head of tubular flowers, pretty pink to bluish purple or sometimes off-white. Purplish papery bracts subtend the flower heads. The simple lance shaped leaves, ½ to 1½ inches long, are opposite and sessile or nearly so on the stems. They have a strong minty odor when crushed. July and August for this one. HABITAT: Gravelly ridge tops or rocky slopes from high plains to open subalpine woods and lower alpine reaches. RANGE: Idaho and E Washington to W Wyoming, New Mexico, and S California.

Mint Family *(Labiatae)*

St. Johnswort Family *(Hypericaceae)*

WESTERN ST. JOHNSWORT

Hypericum formosum HBK. A low spreading perennial, often mat forming, sends up many slender upright stems to 8 inches tall. The shiny green, oval, and sessile leaves attach in opposite pairs. They show tiny purple spots near the smooth margins. The flowers, about ½ inch across, sprout from the axils of the uppermost leaves and display five wide-spreading petals and a multitude of stamens, all brilliant yellow. The buds, often tinged bright red when present, contrast delightfully with the opened flowers, which appear throughout the summer. HABITAT: The seacoast to high alpine. RANGE: Montana to Mexico and west to the coast.

Bladderwort Family *(Lentibulariaceae)*

COMMON BUTTERWORT

Pinguicula vulgaris L. These lovely, solitary, blue-violet flowers on slender unbranched stems, 2 to 5 inches tall, resemble violets at first glance. Of the five unequal petal lobes, the lower one projects outward the farthest. The floral tube extends backward into a narrow cone or spur. Two-inch-long leaves form a basal rosette. Sticky glands cover these pale green or yellowish leaves and small insects stick to them. Enzymes in the sticky exudate digest the insects and extract their juices, leaving only insect skeletons behind. Because the water in high mountains, especially near snow banks, lacks minerals and nutrients, the plant uses insects to supplement its nutrient needs. Look for this fascinating little carnivore in midsummer. HABITAT: Wet mossy seeps and bogs from high montane to alpine. RANGE: Circumpolar, south to Montana and N California. Rare throughout much of its range.

Evening Primrose Family *(Onagraceae)*

RED WILLOWHERB, Alpine Fireweed

Epilobium latifolium L. Gorgeous four-petaled, magenta or occasionally albino flowers welcome the alpine explorer. Three to 12 flowers originate in the axils of the uppermost leaves and form a raceme on reddish branch ends. The plants, either upright or reclining, produce 4 to 16 inch stems. A fine blue glaucus coating tints the oval leaves. They flower through the summer. HABITAT: Scree slopes, gravel bars and stream banks, alpine and subalpine. RANGE: Arctic regions and high mountains, south to Colorado and the Sierras. COMMENT: Common Fireweed, a near relative, stands 4 to 7 feet tall and serves as a valuable nurse plant on burned-over land.

Evening Primrose Family *(Onagraceae)*

ALPINE WILLOWHERB

Epilobium alpinum L. *Epilobium anagallidifolium* Lam. This low plant usually rises less than 1 foot high and spreads by stolons or aerial runners. It may send up one flowering stem or several in a spreading clump. Oval leaves, sessile or nearly so, grow mostly opposite on the stems. Four pink, magenta or white petals open about ¼ inch wide. Rounded lobes cleave the ends of the petals, which sit atop a relatively long, dark brown or purple, tubular ovary. They appear from mid- to late summer. HABITAT: Moist meadows and open slopes from subalpine to alpine. RANGE: Hemispheric, mostly in the mountains, south in the Rockies to Colorado.

Evening Primrose Family *(Onagraceae)*

ROCK FRINGE, Rock Rose

Epilobium obcordatum Gray. These rosy pink to magenta trumpets flare to four petals, rather deeply notched at the tips. The prostrate plants creep over rocks and gravelly slopes, frequently forming mats and spreading by layering. Small oval leaves, covered with a bluish glaucus coating, clothe the slender stems. This unforgettable alpine beauty blooms mostly in August. HABITAT: Alpine meadows and rocky hillsides near or above timberline. RANGE: Bighorn Crags and Sawtooths of Idaho to NE Oregon, Nevada and the Sierras.

57

Phlox Family *(Polemoniaceae)*

ALPINE COLLOMIA

Collomia debilis (Wats.) Greene. These breathtaking little trumpets, ½ to 1 inch long, may vary from white to pink, blue, or even lavender. They nestle amongst matted leaves that may also vary from entire to deeply lobed. Several stems spread around and over rocks and gravel from a deep taproot crown. One may find them blooming in the summer. HABITAT: Rocky talus slopes at alpine elevations. RANGE: Western Wyoming to Utah, Nevada, NE Oregon, and W Montana. Also in the Washington Cascades. COMMENT: We have three varieties in the Rockies, one at lower altitudes.

PYGMY POPPY, Alpine Poppy

Papaver pygmaeum Rydb. Delightful little poppies about ½ inch across, bright orange on the ends of the petals, shade to yellow at the base. Many yellow stamens beautify the center. The plant grows in a tuft from a taproot crown with numerous crowded leaves at the base. The oval leaf blades are less than 1 inch long and deeply dissected into 5 or 7 rounded lobes and quite bristly hairy. They bloom in July and August. HABITAT: Alpine talus slopes. RANGE: A local endemic, limited to Glacier-Waterton International Peace Parks. COMMENT: Another alpine poppy with pale yellow blossoms, *P. kluanense*, occurs in Alberta and the central Rockies. Both species are considered rare and possibly endangered.

Poppy Family *(Papaveraceae)*

Phlox Family *(Polemoniaceae)*

NUTTALL'S LINANTHASTRUM

Linanthastrum nuttallii (Gray) Ewan. Clusters of white sessile trumpets emit a strong, pleasing fragrance from June to August. They crowd the ends of numerous slender stems that straggle along the ground or stand about 1 foot tall. Five bright yellow stamens accent the throat of each floral tube. Pairs of opposite leaves, deeply lobed and sessile, look like whorls of linear leaves. HABITAT: Rocky slopes from high montane to alpine. RANGE: Northeastern Oregon to Montana and south to New Mexico, also in the Cascades and Sierras.

59

Phlox Family *(Polemoniaceae)*

Phlox Family *(Polemoniaceae)*

JACOB'S LADDER, Showy Polemonium, Skunkleaf

Polemonium pulcherrimum var. *pulch.* Hook. These tempting blossoms exhibit five wide-spreading or shallowly cupped petals, pale blue to purple, and a white or yellow throat. Typically the white stamens protrude well beyond the petals. These small plants normally do not rise more than 8 inches high. The pinnately compound leaves have about 20 oval leaflets, ¼ inch long, ranked so uniformly they resemble ladders. They emit a fetid odor, mildly suggestive of skunk, but not particularly noticeable out of doors. Look for Jacob's Ladder from May to July. HABITAT: Alpine and subalpine. RANGE: N Utah to Wyoming and north to the Arctic. COMMENT: Another, more robust variety prefers forested habitats at lower elevation.

SKY PILOT, Sticky Polemonium

Polemonium viscosum Nutt. At the peak of blooming these funnel or bell shaped flowers, arranged in crowded heads, simply sparkle in matchless, incredible shades of blue. Five orange or yellow stamens contrast elegantly with the petals. The plant sends out many branches, 6 to 12 inches high. The leaves are pinnately compound and the leaflets divide palmately, presenting the appearance of leaf whorls. Sticky glandular hairs clothe the leaves and smell somewhat like a skunk. Blooming occurs from June to August. HABITAT: Rocky alpine slopes and ridges. RANGE: Alberta and E Washington to Arizona and New Mexico.

Wild Buckwheat Family *(Polygonaceae)*

GOLDEN BUCKWHEAT

Eriogonum chrysops Rydb. Attractive ball-like heads of yellow flowers, sometimes tinged with red and ⅓ to ⅔ inches across, perch on top of leafless stems ½ to 3 inches tall. Unopened buds lend rich reddish accents to the silvery hairy plants. Small spatula-shaped leaves are densely covered with the woolly hairs. Midsummer is the time to expect their blooming. HABITAT: Mountain slopes from low to alpine heights. RANGE: Idaho, W Montana, and NE Oregon. COMMENT: We have at least three other very similar species of Wild Buckwheat in parts or all of our area.

Wild Buckwheat Family *(Polygonaceae)*

CUSHION BUCKWHEAT, Oval Leaved Eriogonum

Eriogonum ovalifolium Nutt. Silvery hairs cover one or both sides of tiny oval or spatula-shaped leaves that crowd together in spreading mats. Unbranched stems rise only 1 to 3 inches, because alpine sites dwarf this species considerably. Stems lacking leaves or bracts below the inflorescence identify the species. The flowers in dense round umbels, about 1 inch in diameter, are cream or yellow in their prime, depending on the variety. It blooms in July and August turning red or purple with age. HABITAT: From low prairie to alpine. RANGE: Widespread in western U.S. and SW Canada.

61

Wild Buckwheat Family *(Polygonaceae)*

ALPINE BUCKWHEAT, Oarleaf Eriogonum

Eriogonum pyrolaefolium Hook. From a woody taproot crown spreads a small cushion of smooth oval leaves. Several floral stems, unbranched and without stem leaves, recline outward among the leaves. Two linear, leafy bracts subtend each flowering head of white to pinkish, cup shaped blossoms, accented exquisitely with dark purple stamens. Blooming occurs in July and August. HABITAT: Open subalpine forest to rocky alpine heights. RANGE: Western Montana and Idaho to Washington and California.

Wild Buckwheat Family *(Polygonaceae)*

Wild Buckwheat Family *(Polygonaceae)*

ALPINE SORREL

Oxyria digyna (L.) Hill. This high mountain species looks like Dock, *Rumex spp.*
The leaves, which are smooth and
round or kidney shaped, set it apart.
Several stems grow in a cluster and the
long stemmed leaves are mostly basal.
One does not notice the green or
reddish, inconspicuous flowers, but the
flat, oval, winged fruit, either green or
bright red, attract attention in mid- to
late summer. HABITAT: Rocky crevices
and talus slopes where some moisture
occurs. RANGE: Arctic and alpine
areas of the northern hemisphere.
COMMENT: A unique and very common alpine inhabitant that should not
be mistaken for any other.

ALPINE BISTORT, Serpentgrass

Polygonum viviparum L. A smaller
version of Bistort, with a narrow cylin-
drical inflorescence. Minute flowers
along the upper stem may be white or
pink and ordinarily sterile. Lower on the
stem one finds tiny pink to dark purple
bulblets that reproduce the plant
vegetatively. One to several simple
stems originate on a woody root crown.
Most of the leaves grow from the base
and have narrowly oval blades on rather
long petioles, while a few stem leaves
grow much smaller and sessile upward.
Flowers appear in summer. HABITAT:
Moist places from subalpine woods to
lofty alpine reaches. RANGE: Much of
the mountainous northern hemisphere.

Wild Buckwheat Family *(Polygonaceae)*

AMERICAN BISTORT, Bottle Brush

Polygonum bistortoides Pursh. A thick mass of tiny individual flowers create cheerful white or reddish heads. Eight stamens protrude from each blossom and impart a ragged, bristly look to the inflorescence. Several slender stems rise 8 to 24 inches from a thick edible root. Large oblong leaves also shoot up from the root on long petioles. A few small, sessile leaves sheath the stem. Blooming occurs from June to August. HABITAT: Meadows and other moist places from valleys to alpine regions. RANGE: Western U.S. and Canada. COMMENT: Very common and frequently abundant, they sometimes turn meadows snowy white.

ALPINE SPRING BEAUTY

Claytonia megarhiza (Gray) Parry. This delicate alpine beauty richly rewards the climber who will seek it out. It has five white to rosy pink petals striped with red. The plant grows in a tuft, radiating several to many floral stems around or among the leaves. Numerous rounded leaves, somewhat leathery, succulent, and smooth to the touch, create a shiny basal rosette. Its woody root, that approaches 1 inch in thickness, immediately identifies this species. Look for it in summer. HABITAT: Rocky or gravelly slopes and rock crevices above or near timberline. RANGE: Southern Alberta to E Washington and New Mexico. COMMENT: Alpine Spring Beauty should be considered rare and left undisturbed. The flowers appear nearly identical to the common Western Spring Beauty, shown in Vol. II, *Forest Wildflowers.*.

Purslane Family *(Portulacaceae)*

Purslane Family *(Portulacaceae)*

PUSSYPAWS

Spraguea umbellata Torr. *Calyptridium umbellatum* Greene. Charming ball-like heads of pink or white flowers usually spread along the ground. On close examination one finds two round papery and persistent sepals tightly clasping narrower petals that wither early. Some magnification greatly improves one's appreciation of this intricate flower structure. The unbranched and naked flower stems spring from basal rosettes of smooth club shaped leaves, ½ to 2 inches long. Pussypaws may be annuals at lower elevations and perennials at high altitudes. Blooming occurs from early to midsummer. HABITAT: Sandy or gravelly sites from open montane to alpine. RANGE: Western Montana to Utah and west to the coast, B.C. to Baja.

Purslane Family *(Portulacaceae)*

PYGMY BITTERROOT

Lewisia pygmaea var. *pygmaea* (Gray) Robins. These exquisite little flowers usually possess seven bright pink, but occasionally white, petals. One or several flower stems nestle in the leaves. A single blossom graces each stem. The linear fleshy leaves stay green through the blooming period in midsummer. HABITAT: Gravelly slopes and ridges in subalpine and alpine regions. RANGE: Mountains of western United States and Canada. COMMENT: Pictures of Bitterroot, the state flower of Montana, and Nevada Pygmy Bitterroot appear in Vol. I, *Prairie Wildflowers.*.

FEW FLOWERED SHOOTING STAR

Dodecatheon pulchellum (Raf.) Merrill. This beautiful wildflower looks like a small colorful rocket. The yellow and purplish-black stamens fuse together around the style to form the nose, while the pink to intensely magenta petals flare backward into a spreading tail. A few flowers in an umbel decorate the top of one or more smooth stems. Several shiny green leaves create a basal rosette. This species varies widely and botanists have given it many scientific names. It blooms early in the spring at low elevations to midsummer above timberline. HABITAT: Generally damp locations. RANGE: Widespread throughout the west. COMMENT: We have several different species in the Rockies including at least one white one.

Primrose Family *(Primulaceae)*

Primrose Family *(Primulaceae)*

ROCK JASMINE

Androsace chamaejasme Wulf. Breathtaking clusters of little white flowers with yellow or pink eyes, they remind one of forget-me-nots. Each plant sends slender branches along the ground and produces a rosette of tiny, copiously hairy leaves at the end of each branch. The flower stem is also hairy. A tight raceme of 2 to 8 flowers tops the stem. This one blooms in June and July. HABITAT: Gravelly slopes to rock crevices, mostly alpine. RANGE: An arctic plant of Asia and North America, south through the Rockies to Colorado.

Primrose Family *(Primulaceae)*

FAIRY PRIMROSE, Alpine Primrose

Primula angustifolia Torr. Gaudy little flowers grow singly or a few per plant. The five rose petals have small notches at the tip, spreading wide from a short floral tube that displays a pretty 5-sided pattern. One must get down on one's knees, reverently, to fully admire these treasures. They stand only 1 to 3 inches high in a tuft of narrow, entire leaves about 1 inch long. Blooms early in the alpine season in May and early June. HABITAT: High forest to rocky alpine ridge tops and slopes, preferring heights of 12,000 to 13,000 feet. RANGE: Utah, Colorado, and New Mexico. COMMENT: The fairy ring pattern of plants shown in the photograph is not typical of the species—just providential for the photographer. Fairy Primrose is now grown horticulturally. It produces several flowers per stem at low altitudes.

Primrose Family *(Primulaceae)*

PARRY'S PRIMROSE

Primula parryi Gray. The discovery of Parry's Primrose handsomely rewards the high mountain hiker or rock scrambler. Several magenta or purplish-red, bell-shaped flowers with yellow eyes top an upright stem to 10 inches tall. The leaves, which all sprout from the base, also stand upright in a tuft nearly as tall as the flowers. Such vertical nature is unusual for high alpine flora. The flowers emit a rather offensive odor. Look for these spectacular blooms in midsummer. HABITAT: Moist stream banks to open mountain tops and rocky slopes, where they like the drip line of large boulders, taking advantage of rain water runoff; seldom found below 10,000 feet elevation. RANGE: The Rocky Mountains south of Canada.

Buttercup Family *(Ranunculaceae)*

Buttercup Family *(Ranunculaceae)*

WHITE MONKSHOOD

Aconitum columbianum var.
ochroleucum Nels. Commonly the
flowers of monkshood exhibit a deep
blue color, but this creamy variety also
occurs in the Rockies. Unmistakably the
upper sepal forms a hood into which
bees must crawl to reach nectar and
pollen. Two broadly oval sepals spread
wide on the sides and two smaller
narrow sepals droop below. Two small
petals usually blend with the sepals.
The leaves divide palmately and have
numerous teeth on the margins. The
plants stand 1 to 5 feet tall and bloom
in midsummer. HABITAT: Bogs,
meadows, and other moist sites, most
commonly subalpine. RANGE: Eastern
Washington to W Montana and south to
New Mexico.

DRUMMOND'S ANEMONE

Anemone drummondii Wats. One or
two flower stems grow 4 to 10 inches
high. Each stem bears one handsome
white flower about 1 inch across, often
tinged green, blue, or lilac on the back
of the sepals. Most leaves grow in a
basal tuft on long petioles, and a whorl
of sessile leaves circles the stem at
mid height. A leaf usually has three
leaflets, each deeply divided into three
narrow segments. Short straight hairs
coat leaves, stems, and the back of the
sepals. Blooming occurs from May to
July. HABITAT: Meadows and slopes
from high montane to alpine. RANGE:
Montana to Alaska and the Sierras.

Buttercup Family *(Ranunculaceae)*   **Seed head**

WESTERN PASQUEFLOWER

Anemone occidentalis Wats. Large solitary white to pale blue flowers, 2 to 2½ inches in diameter, rest on the ends of short stems that continue to rise up to 20 inches in fruit. A halo of yellow stamens surrounds a central mass of greenish pistils. The basal leaves have long petioles, while those growing in a whorl on the stem are short petioled. Many linear segments divide the compound leaves. These engaging blossoms may emerge early or late in the season. HABITAT: Meadows and hillsides in fairly deep soil at subalpine elevations and upward. RANGE: Montana to E Oregon and the Sierras and north through British Columbia and Alberta. COMMENT: Because the flowers normally open before the leaves, in early bloom it can be mistaken for Globeflower, p. 77, but the leaves are diagnostic.

PACIFIC ANEMONE, Cliff Anemone

Anemone multifida Poir. Similar to Drummond's Anemone, but ordinarily taller with smaller flowers and sometimes with three flowers per stem, originating in the axils of a central leaf whorl. The colorful sepals vary from cream to yellow to red, sometimes in combinations of these colors on one plant. Blooms appear from early in the season to August. HABITAT: Open slopes and rocky places from medium elevations to alpine. RANGE: The cold regions of the Americas from the arctic to the Straits of Magellan. COMMENT: We have three varieties of Pacific Anemone and two other species that could easily be mistaken for this one or Drummond's Anemone.

Buttercup Family *(Ranunculaceae)*

Buttercup Family *(Ranunculaceae)*

NORTHERN or ARCTIC ANEMONE

Anemone parviflora Michx. These small anemones show just one flower on a single stem and usually stand no more than 4 inches tall. They spread by underground rhizomes. Basal leaves in a small clump divide palmately into three main lobes that have shallow scallops on the end. One whorl of nearly sessile stem leaves divides almost to the base. White flowers with greenish centers predominate, but bluish tinged sepals are not uncommon. The flowers may open from May to August. HABITAT: Open subalpine woods to alpine meadows and slopes. RANGE: Alaska and much of Canada, south to NW Washington, NE Oregon, and Colorado; also in Asia.

Buttercup Family *(Ranunculaceae)*

YELLOW COLUMBINE, Golden Columbine

Aquilegia flavescens Wats. This resplendent columbine normally exhibits two delicate shades of yellow, especially in alpine habitats, but a red one is shown in Vol. II, *Forest Wildflowers*. The petal spurs, about ½ inch long, are considerably shorter than Colorado Columbine and they curve inward in graceful coils. In other respects the two species are quite similar. This one blooms typically in summer. HABITAT: Meadows and moist hillsides from mid montane to alpine terrain, commonly frequenting alpine cirques. RANGE: Most of the northern Rockies and Washington Cascades. COMMENT: From Colorado into New Mexico *A. flavescens* gives way to another yellow columbine, *A. chrysantha*.

Buttercup Family *(Ranunculaceae)*

Buttercup Family *(Ranunculaceae)*

COLORADO COLUMBINE, Blue Columbine

Aquilegia coerulea James. The glorious blossom shown on the front cover is the state flower of Colorado, where its white petal lobes and ice blue to dark blue sepals and petal spurs make it a memorable treasure. Although blue colored specimens predominate in Colorado, pure white ones occur occasionally. In Wyoming, N Utah, S Montana, and S Idaho one generally finds sheer white or cream colored flowers, variety *ochroleuca,* shown on this page. Each petal projects backward into a tapering spur, 1 to 1½ inches long—the longest of any native columbine. The plants stand 1 to 2 feet tall. Most of the leaves attach at the base. They have compound segments with irregular, rounded lobes. Blooms appear from early to midsummer. HABITAT: Woods, meadows, and open rocky slopes from mid montane to high alpine. RANGE: Southwestern Montana and S Idaho to Arizona and New Mexico. COMMENT: Many varieties have been developed for the perennial gardener through selection and hybridization.

RED COLUMBINE, Sitka Columbine

Aquilegia formosa Fisch. A gaudy columbine with straight spurs nods gently in mountain breezes. The five petals show brickred spurs on one end, attach to the sepals in the middle, and flare to broad yellow lobes on the other end. Five red sepals alternate with the petals. In other respects the plants are very similar to *A. flavescens.* The tips of the spurs hold nectar, which only long-tongued moths, butterflies, or hummingbirds can reach. Blooming continues through the summer months. HABITAT: Highly variable from seashore to mostly subalpine in the Rockies. RANGE: Most of western North America.

74

Buttercup Family *(Ranunculaceae)*

JONES COLUMBINE, Limestone Columbine

Aquilegia jonesii Parry. Rare but not endangered, this indescribably blue columbine compares favorably in size with other species, but the spurs project backward only about ¼ inch. The plants only grow 1 to 4 inches high in a dense mass of small leaves with many oval lobes that do not lie flat. Look for this gorgeous wildflower mainly in June or early July. HABITAT: Restricted to limestone talus slopes or outcrops above timberline. RANGE: The Rocky Mountain crest from S Alberta to Wyoming. COMMENT: Jones Columbine will flourish only in its preferred habitat and does not long survive transplanting. Enjoy it in its lofty native home and leave it for others to savor.

Buttercup Family *(Ranunculaceae)*

Buttercup Family *(Ranunculaceae)*

MARSH MARIGOLD Cowslip, Elk's Lip
Caltha leptosepala DC. Alpine meadows flooded with early season runoff sometimes sparkle with masses of Marsh Marigold. The low plants ordinarily bear just one flower, 1½ to 2 inches across, graced by many yellow stamens. The leaves are roundly heart-shaped and slightly scalloped on the margins. They emerge from the base of the plant. It blooms very early in the season to midsummer. HABITAT: Wet meadows and shorelines, subalpine and alpine. RANGE: Western United States and Canada, including Alaska. COMMENT: A similar species, *C. biflora*, also occurs in Colorado and Utah and mountains of the west coast. Sometimes Marsh Marigold intermixes with Globeflower, which see, and blooms at the same time.

BARBEY'S DELPHINIUM Subalpine Larkspur
Delphinium barbeyi Huth. These tall straight plants, 2 to 5 feet, produce a short inflorescence of crowded navy blue to purplish flowers, composed of five sepals that flare widely. The upper sepal extends backward into a grace-fully curving, conical spur nearly 1 inch long. The flowers have four small petals, the upper pair creating white accents against the dark colorful sepals. Palmately compound leaves grow mostly on the stem, the segments narrrow at the point of attachment. It blooms in summer. HABITAT: Subalpine hillsides, meadows, and stream banks, preferring well protected locations. RANGE: Wyoming and Utah to New Mexico and Arizona. COMMENT: Western Delphinium, *D. occidentale*, usually stands 5 to 7 feet tall, ranges farther north and carries smaller, more widely spaced flowers that tend to pale blue.

Buttercup Family *(Ranunculaceae)*

GLOBEFLOWER

Trollius laxus Salisb. This memorable plant sends up several stems in a clump, 4 to 12 inches high. A solitary flower, about 1½ inches in diameter, terminates each stem and consists of five or more white, cream, or pale yellow sepals. In the northern part of its range, white flowers predominate while pale yellowish ones occur more commonly to the south. Numerous yellow stamens embellish the center. Minute linear petals form a ring around the stamens and usually go unnoticed.

The leaves divide palmately into five lobes, each one further lobed irregularly. Three leaves usually attach to each stem, the upper one closely subtending the flower. They open soon after snow melt. HABITAT: Wet woods, meadows, and stream banks, subalpine and alpine. RANGE: British Columbia and Alberta, south to Washington and Colorado. Also rare in NE states, Michigan to Connecticut. COMMENT: Can be mistaken for Western Pasqueflower, p. 71 or Marsh Marigold, p. 76.

Buttercup Family *(Ranunculaceae)*

PLANTAIN LEAVED BUTTERCUP

Ranunculus alismaefolius var. *montanus*
Wats. On each plant several bright
yellow buttercups ordinarily possess ten
narrow petals. They perch atop stems
that branch from upper leaf axils. The
plants stand 4 to 10 inches tall and
support entire, lance-shaped leaves,
prominently parallel veined. The leaves
resemble those of common plantain
and readily distinguish this buttercup.
Blooms late spring to summer.
HABITAT: High mountain meadows and
moist woods to alpine. RANGE: S Idaho
and S Wyoming to Colorado and Utah.
COMMENT: Several other varieties,
mostly with five petals, range throughout W United States and Canada.

Buttercup Family *(Ranunculaceae)*

Buttercup Family *(Ranunculaceae)*

SNOW BUTTERCUP

Ranunculus adoneus Gray. A brilliantly yellow or yellowish-orange buttercup bears one to three flowers about ¾ inch in diameter per stem. Beneath the petals purple tinges color the sepals. Several stems grow in a tuft and the leaves usually divide into six threadlike segments. Snow Buttercup blooms as soon as the snow melts, even beginning to open under the snow and sometimes poking through the last fringe of retreating snow drifts. . HABITAT: Alpine slopes and cirques. RANGE: Colorado to Nevada, S Idaho, and Wyoming.

ALPINE BUTTERCUP

Ranunculus eschscholtzii Schlect. These smooth perky little plants have one to three blossoms each. Several or many of them often grow in masses on favorable sites. Five waxy yellow petals, about ½ inch long, and numerous yellow or greenish stamens adorn each flower. Most of the glossy green leaves spring from the base of the plants on slender petioles. They show three palmate lobes, parted more than halfway to the base and the lobes may be roundly scalloped. Look for these beauties in early summer. HABITAT: Wet stream banks, meadows, and slopes in alpine country. RANGE: Mountains of western North America, north of Mexico. COMMENT: One can find more than 30 species of buttercup in our area incuding about a dozen at alpine elevations.

YELLOW MOUNTAIN AVENS

Dryas drummondii Richards. Yellow Mountain Avens, a semishrub, forms a loose spreading ground cover. The flowers sit more or less horizontally on short upright stems, 2 to 10 inches tall. They normally have seven pretty, tightly cupped petals and many yellow stamens. The evergreen leaves of *Dryas* are quite distinctive. About 1 inch long and narrowly oval or lance shaped, they exhibit scallops on the surface between prominent veins and edges that curl under. They are bright green above and silvery hairy underneath. The blossoms open from mid May to July. HABITAT: Gravel bars along streams at medium and subalpine elevations to rocky, gravelly sites in alpine terrain. RANGE: Montana to NE Oregon and north to Alaska. COMMENT: In fruit the styles persist and elongate to feathery tails that help the seeds carry on the wind.

Rose Family *(Rosaceae)*

Rose Family *(Rosaceae)*

WHITE MOUNTAIN AVENS, Dryad

Dryas octopetala L. A low mat-forming semishrub with white flowers, about 1½ inches in diameter, perched slightly above or nestled among the leaves. Each flower normally displays eight petals (*octopetala*) and many yellow stamens. The leaves are similar to *D. drummondii*, but somewhat narrower. Look for them in early summer. HABITAT: Common on high windswept slopes and mountain tops, but also on gravel bars at subalpine altitudes. RANGE: Arctic regions of the northern hemisphere, south to Colorado and Washington.

IVESIA

Ivesia gordonii (Hook.) T. & G. To be fully appreciated, these dainty little blossoms require magnification. Several to many flowers form ball-like heads about ¾ inch in diameter terminating stems 2 to 6 inches tall. The individual flowers have five sharp, pointed, star like sepals alternating with five shorter rounded petals and five stamens, all in various shades of yellow. The narrow fern-like leaves are 1 to 3 inches long, composed of more than 20 tiny leaflets, each one lobed several times. These delicate blooms appear in June and July. HABITAT: Gravelly places, high montane to alpine. RANGE: Northern Rocky Mountain states, the Cascades, and Sierras. COMMENT: One other alpine *Ivesia* reaches our region from Canada.

Rose Family *(Rosaceae)*

Rose Family *(Rosaceae)*

ALPINE AVENS

Geum rossii (R.Br.) Ser. One of the most common alpine inhabitants looks like Cinquefoil or *Potentilla*, which see, and differs only on technical characters. The plant reaches 4 to 12 inches high and forms dense mats or solid turf on favorable sites. Many pinnate lobes that do not lie flat identify the 2- to 4-inch leaves. In late summer and fall the leaves turn red or bronze and may color whole mountain sides. The flowers open mostly in midsummer, but some may continue into early fall. HABITAT: Alpine slopes, meadows and tundra. RANGE: Alaska to Arizona and New Mexico and in Asia.

Rose Family *(Rosaceae)*

KELSEYA

Kelseya uniflora (Wats.) Rydb. Kelseya is the floral emblem of the Montana Native Plant Society and a long-lived perennial. This unique plant grows only on limestone rock, usually on the face of a cliff. The roots penetrate cracks in the rocks, while the aerial portion forms a dense cushion up to 2 or 3 inches thick and 1½ feet in diameter against the face of the cliff. Stems about 1 to 2 inches long are tightly packed and densely covered with overlapping leaves, on the order of ¹⁄₁₆ inch long. Dead leaves persist on the stems, adding to the cushion effect of the plant. Silky hairs impart a velvety, grey-green tint to the leaves. Tiny pink to reddish purple flowers ¹⁄₁₆ to ⅛ inch across and solitary on the stem ends gaily dot the cushions from April to June. HABITAT: Limestone cliffs from 4,400 to 11,500 feet elevation. RANGE: Idaho, Montana, and Wyoming. COMMENT: Because of its stringent growth requirements, *Kelseya* does not transplant or propagate easily. Rare but not endangered.

PARTRIDGEFOOT, Meadow Spiraea

Luetkea pectinata (Pursh) Kuntze.
Occasionally one encounters a wildflower so captivating that the memory
lingers long after many others are
forgotten. Partridgefoot can cast such a
spell for the alpine hiker. The tiny white
flowers form a tight cluster atop a 2 to
6 inch stem. Yellow eyes gleam from
the floral centers. The leaves, deeply
parted into linear segments remind one
of birds' tracks in the dust or snow.
They sometimes create dense mats,
since the plants spread by stolons,
usually on fairly deep soil. Search for
this choice alpine in summer. HABITAT:
Meadows and slopes, often in snow
retention areas, subalpine and alpine.
RANGE: Alaska to Idaho, Montana, and
N California. COMMENT: *Luetkea* has
just one species.

Rose Family *(Rosaceae)*

Rose Family *(Rosaceae)*

ROCKMAT

Petrophytum caespitosum (Nutt.) Rydb.
Well drained rock crevices from cliff
faces to ridge tops provide a footing
for Rockmat. Strong woody roots
penetrate deep into rocks. The surface
plant makes a dense mat up to 3 feet
across. Spatula shaped leaves, to ½
inch long, carry a grey-green coating
and a few fine hairs. Flowering stems
rise 1 to 4 inches, the ends covered
with tiny white flowers and bristling
stamens. Blooms mostly in August.
HABITAT: Limestone or granite rock
outcrops from low to alpine elevations.
RANGE: South Dakota to NE Oregon,
California, and Texas.

SHRUBBY CINQUEFOIL, Potentilla

Potentilla fruticosa L. Handsome bushy shrubs, 1 to 4 feet tall, bear solitary flowers about 1 inch across, or small clusters in leaf axils. Five broad petals radiate outward from a mass of similarly colored stamens. The pinnate leaves spread five (3 to 7) narrow linear leaflets about ½ inch long. Silky hairs impart a grey-green cast to the leaves. Blossoms first appear in early summer. HABITAT: Open woods and meadows in the mountains to alpine heights. RANGE: Cold, mostly mountainous, regions of the northern hemisphere. COMMENT: Called "Potentilla" by the trade, it has become a widely planted ornamental.

Rose Family *(Rosaceae)*

Rose Family *(Rosaceae)*

SNOW CINQUEFOIL, Alpine Potentilla

Potentilla nivea L. Five broad yellow petals, shallowly lobed on the end, surround a mound of yellow stamens and pistils. Stems 1½ to 6 inches tall may bear 1 to 9 flowers in a sparingly branched inflorescence. The leaves, palmately 3-lobed and toothed, erupt mainly from the base of the plant, are greenish above and silvery hairy on the underside. Look for it in June and July. HABITAT: Gravelly places or alpine meadows in lofty mountains. RANGE: Circumpolar at arctic latitudes and south in high mountains to Utah and Colorado. COMMENT: Oneflowered Cinquefoil, *P. uniflora*, as well as several other species, exhibit characteristics similar to this one.

Rose Family *(Rosaceae)*

Willow Family *(Salicaceae)*

CREEPING SIBBALDIA

Sibbaldia procumbens L. Very common at high altitudes but inconspicuous and often unnoticed, this small creeping mat former likes to invade bare or disturbed ground. The leaves sprout mostly from horizontal stems. They are palmately 3-lobed and resemble strawberry leaves. Five minute rounded yellow petals alternate with five longer, pointed green sepals. Five stamens, unusual for members of the rose family, compliment the floral center. Flowering occurs in summer. HABITAT: Well drained meadows and alpine slopes. RANGE: circumpolar; most of Canada, south to Colorado, Utah, and California.

SNOW WILLOW

Salix nivalis Hook. In high alpine areas one may find a willow that spreads along the ground, no more than 4 inches high, by woody rhizomes at or just below the ground. Oval, rounded leaves about 1 inch long spring from the prostrate stems. The leaves show a prominent network of veins, bright green surfaces above and woolly hairy undersides. Greenish-yellow, unisexual catkins terminate the current year's growth from mid- to late summer. HABITAT: Meadows and rocky or gravelly slopes. RANGE: Canada to California and New Mexico. COMMENT: A total of four low, prostrate willow species inhabit our alpine fastnesses. All of them provide important winter food for ptarmigan.

Rose Family *(Rosaceae)*

PINK SPIRAEA, Subalpine Spiraea

Spiraea densiflora Nutt. These low shrubs, 2 to 4 feet high, create dazzling rose-pink floral displays. The individual flowers are tiny, about ⅛ inch long, but they form dense, flat topped or rounded clusters, 1 to 3 inches across. They add a very pleasant fragrance to high mountain air. Many projecting stamens make them appear quite fuzzy. Bright green oval leaves with fine teeth on the upper half of the margins cover the many stems. The blossoms open in July. HABITAT: Subalpine stream banks, lake shores, and alpine cirques. RANGE: British Columbia to Montana, Wyoming, and California. COMMENT: Two other species of pink flowered *Spiraea* enhance the beauty of the Rockies.

Saxifrage Family *(Saxifragaceae)*

Saxifrage Family *(Saxifragaceae)*

GOOSEBERRY LEAVED ALUMROOT

Heuchera grossulariifolia Rydb. Leafless stems, 6 to 24 inches, erupt from a basal tuft of roundly heart shaped leaves that are shallowly lobed numerous times. Cup shaped or tubular flowers crowd the stem tip. Five tiny white petals perch on long stalks from the base and expand (oar shaped) at the tip. They peek out of the calyx cup, while five stamens hide within the cup. May to August. HABITAT: Lower elevation hillsides to rocky alpine slopes. RANGE: Western Montana to Oregon and Washington.

COMMON ALUMROOT, Small Leaved Alumroot

Heuchera parvifolia Nutt. The leaves of this alumroot also grow in a basal tuft. Stems may rise 6 to 24 inches. The numerous flowers group tightly at first, but the stem continues to elongate as the season advances, so that the inflorescence may stretch ten inches as in the photograph. The flower base is green and conic below and saucer shaped on top. Five tiny rounded petals protrude from a short stalked base in the summer. HABITAT: Gravel, rocky places and on cliffs, montane to subalpine. RANGE: Alberta to Mexico through the Rockies.

Saxifrage Family *(Saxifragaceae)*

FRINGED GRASS OF PARNASSUS

Parnassia fimbriata Konig. This sheer white, five-petaled charmer is unmistakable and unforgettable. Prominent hair-like fringes decorate the narrowed bases of the petals. Solitary saucer-shaped flowers about 1 inch in diameter, terminate smooth slender stems 4 to 12 inches tall. Glossy green, heart-shaped or kidney-shaped leaves emerge from the base of the plant on short petioles. One small smooth leaf clasps the stem at mid height as it blooms in the middle of summer. HABITAT: Common on mossy banks and other wet places from middle ` elevations to alpine. RANGE: The Rockies and Sierras to Alaska. COMMENT: One can find three other species of *Parnassia* in our area, but they lack the fringed petals that distinguish this one so markedly.

BROOK SAXIFRAGE

Saxifraga arguta Don. Naked flower stems rise from a mass of shiny green leaves at mossy brook side. The miniature flowers spread five white petals while pretty red stamens, ovaries, and unopened buds provide exquisite accents. The round leaves are deeply indented or toothed on the margins. These alluring little flowers bloom in mid- and late summer. HABITAT: Edges of water courses from forests to alpine. RANGE: Mountains of W North America. COMMENT: Twenty species of *Saxifraga* occur in the Rockies, at least 18 of them in the alpine flora.

Saxifrage Family *(Saxifragaceae)*

Saxifrage Family *(Saxifragaceae)*

SPOTTED SAXIFRAGE

Saxifraga bronchialis L. Five small white petals, gorgeously stippled in colors of the spectrum from red to orange to yellow, form a shallow saucer, supporting a superior white ovary. The plants may be tufted, but more commonly make dense mats. Numerous branching flower stems rise from the mats to 6 inches high. Needle-shaped leaves, ¼ to ½ inch long, clothe the prostrate stems and may remain attached for several years. They bloom from late spring to midsummer. HABITAT: Rocky or gravelly sites, seashore to high alpine. RANGE: Circumpolar in the arctic, south to New Mexico.

Saxifrage Family *(Saxifragaceae)*

Saxifrage Family *(Saxifragaceae)*

PURPLE SAXIFRAGE, Twinleaf Saxifrage

Saxifraga oppositifolia L. Another dense cushion plant only 1 or 2 inches high, bears glorious purple or wine-colored flowers. The rounded petals are about ¼ to ⅜ inch long and create blossoms surprisingly large for the rest of the plant. Many prostrate stems spread from the root crown. Rounded leaves only about ⅛ inch long grow opposite on the stems so tightly spaced that they overlap like shingles. Short straight hairs line the leaf margins. Purple Saxifrage blooms very early in the alpine season. HABITAT: Rocky talus slopes and exposed ridges and rock outcrops above timberline. RANGE: Circumpolar in the arctic and south in high mountains to Washington, NE Oregon, Idaho, and Wyoming.

ALPINE BOG SAXIFRAGE

Saxifraga oregana var. *subapetala* (Nels.) Hitchc. These unusual alpine flowers show only vestiges of petals or lack them altogether. Several other varieties of Bog Saxifrage display petals of normal size for the genus at lower elevations. In this variety the sepals, stamens, and fruit all assume various shades of purple. The leafless stems stand 6 to 12 inches tall above a rosette of lance shaped basal leaves. They bloom from mid- to late summer. HABITAT: Bogs, meadows, and stream banks at high altitudes. RANGE: Colorado and Utah, northward through the Rockies.

TELESONIX, James' Saxifrage

Telesonix jamesii (Torr.) Raf. Five pink to purplish, widely spaced petals, rounded on the ends but narrowed to slender stalks, mark the seductive little Telesonix. The petals spring from the lip of a reddish purple, bell shaped calyx. Several to many flowers embellish a few scattered stems, 2 to 8 inches high, also tinged with reddish coloration and generously clothed with short, sticky-glandular hairs. The leaves mostly grow in a basal clump and are heart- or kidney-shaped and generously toothed on the margins. Dead leaves from previous years often persist at the base. *Telesonix* has just one species, but two varieties grace the Rockies. Blooms open in midsummer. HABITAT: Rock crevices and talus slopes, usually on moist, north facing exposures. RANGE: Alberta to Colorado, Utah, and Nevada.

Saxifrage Family *(Saxifragaceae)*

Saxifrage Family *(Saxifragaceae)*

GOLDBLOOM SAXIFRAGE

Saxifraga serpyllifolia ssp. *chrysantha* (Gray) Weber. This tiny alpine habitue produces five brilliant yellow petals, gloriously dotted with several rows of minute orange spots. The stems erupt from a rosette of miniature, almost mosslike leaves. Yellow at first, the central ovary turns bright red when ripe. It blooms in summer. HABITAT: Gravelly ridges, slopes, and mountain tops from 11,000 to 14,000 feet. RANGE: Southeastern Wyoming, NE Utah, and Colorado. COMMENT: Whiplash Saxifrage, *S. flagellaris*, could be mistaken for this one, but it reproduces in part by runners.

WALLOWA MOUNTAIN PAINTBRUSH

Castilleja chrysantha Greenm. Several stems rise in a clump, 4 to 12 inches tall but occasionally to 20 inches, from a woody root. Pale purple splashes sometimes color the greenish-yellow upper bracts. The lower leaves are simple, the upper leaves and bracts 3-lobed. Blooms may occur from early in the season to September. HABITAT: Moist ground in subalpine and alpine zones. RANGE: Limited to the Wallowa and Blue Mountains of NE Oregon and SE Washington. COMMENT: Some species of Indian Paintbrush are root parasites that feed on the roots of other plants.

Figwort Family *(Scrophulariaceae)*

Figwort Family *(Scrophulariaceae)*

Castilleja wallowensis Pennell *C. chrysantha* x *rhexifolia* (Hybrid). Lacking a common name, this lovely, lavender or purplish hybrid displays many of the characteristics of Wallowa Mountain Paintbrush and Rosy Paintbrush. It differs, however, in some characters from both of these parent species. It is generally smaller than either parent. The flower stems grow only about 2 to 4 inches long and are decumbent (not upright) at the base. It blooms in summer. HABITAT: Gravelly, often shifting, alpine slopes. RANGE: apparently limited to the Wallowa mountains of NE Oregon in the Eaglecap Wilderness. COMMENT: Several other low paintbrush species grace our alpine flora.

92

Figwort Family *(Scrophulariaceae)*

ROSY PAINTBRUSH

Castilleja rhexifolia Rydb. Several species of Indian Paintbrush could be called red or rosy in our alpine flora. This one has also been called split-leaf or rhexia leaved, which seems to be a misnomer. The leaves of Rosy Paintbrush are mostly simple and only occasionally split into lobes or segments. The rose (pink to scarlet or even purple) bracts of the inflorescence ordinarily do not split into lobes, as shown in the picture, or have one narrow, linear lobe on each side of the broad central lobe. It blooms in July and August. HABITAT: Subalpine and alpine, meadows and slopes. RANGE: Utah and Colorado to Alberta and the north Cascades of Washington into British Columbia.

SNOWLOVER

Chionophila tweedyi (C & R) Hend. This perky little wraith, closely related to the penstemons, sports four to ten tubular, two-lipped blossoms, all on one side of the 2 to 10 inch tall stem. The lips pinch the tube nearly or completely closed. Delicate pink to pale lavender hues tint the blooms. A few smooth pointed leaves cluster at the base of the plants and one or more miniature grass-like pairs of stem leaves go almost unnoticed. It spreads from underground rhizomes and generally occurs in sparsely scattered colonies. Midsummer is the time to look for this one. HABITAT: Sandy or gravelly soil in scattered subalpine timber to open alpine areas. RANGE: Central Idaho to W Montana. COMMENT: *C. jamesii*, the only other member of the genus, occupies alpine habitat in Colorado and S Wyoming. It is quite rare.

Figwort Family *(Scrophulariaceae)*

Figwort Family *(Scrophulariaceae)*

FEATHERLEAF KITTENTAILS, Cutleaf Synthyris

Synthyris pinnatifida Wats. Dense racemes of intensely blue or purplish flowers stand only about 2 inches at first blooming, but the floral stem may rise to 8 inches at maturity. The leaves, deeply cleft pinnately with sharp pointed lobes, sprout from the base. Blooming occurs early in the alpine season. HABITAT: Rocky or gravelly slopes in subalpine and alpine terrain. RANGE: Central Idaho, SW Montana, Wyoming, and Utah; also the Olympic Mountains of Washington. COMMENT: Could easily be mistaken for *Bessya alpina*, which has lance shaped leaves toothed on the edges.

Figwort Family *(Scrophulariaceae)*

Figwort Family *(Scrophulariaceae)*

LEWIS MONKEYFLOWER

Mimulus lewisii Pursh. A spectacular, rose red, tubular flower, about 1½ inches long, with five spreading petal lobes, two above and three below, and a yellow hairy throat. Stems rise from spreading roots and grow 1 to 3 feet long, upright when short but tending to recline when long or not crowded. They frequently make solid masses of growth in favorable locations. The opposite leaves are broadly lance shaped, sticky, hairy and slightly indented on the margins. It blooms in summer. HABITAT: Wet stream banks and pool edges at high elevations. RANGE: Utah and W Colorado to Alberta, British Columbia, and California. COMMENT: Named for Meriwether Lewis of Lewis and Clark fame.

SUBALPINE MONKEYFLOWER

Mimulus tilingii Regel. A delightful splash of bright yellow on low creeping plants, 2 to 8 inches high, they often grow in masses of vegetation on mossy banks and along rivulets at high attitude. Each upright stem bears about four flowers on pedicels longer than the flowers from axils of the upper leaves. Two ridges of the lower petals, delicately spotted with orange or reddish-brown, nearly close the throat of each blossom. Blooming occurs late in summer. HABITAT: Alpine stream banks. RANGE: The Rocky Mountains and Cascade-Sierras.

Figwort Family *(Scrophulariaceae)*

Figwort Family *(Scrophulariaceae)*

BRACTED LOUSEWORT, Wood Betony

Pedicularis bracteosa Benth. Strange beauty characterizes these flowers that form a dense terminal spike or raceme. Each yellow or reddish-purple blossom has a narrow upper hood that turns downward on the end into a beak. The hood extends over a lower lip, composed of three fused petals. Numerous narrow leafy bracts subtend and intermix with the blossoms. Several unbranched stems, a few inches to 3 feet tall, rise from the root crown, which sends up pinnately compound and sharply toothed leaves. It blooms in summer. HABITAT: Moist soil from mid montane to alpine. RANGE: From Colorado to California and north into Canada. COMMENT: We have five varieties of Bracted Lousewort. Several species of *Pedicularis* are known as semi-root parasites, gaining partial sustenance from other plants through attachment of the roots.

COILED LOUSEWORT, Fernleaf Sickletop

Pedicularis contorta var. *contorta* Benth. Numerous blossoms space themselves openly along the upper half of several slender stems, 6 to 24 inches high. A fascinating upper petal coils gracefully downward, like a sickle, above three lower, fused, lip petals. The leaves, mostly basal, are pinnately lobed into narrow, sharply toothed, fern-like segments. It blooms from June to August. HABITAT: Moist meadows and slopes, most commonly subalpine. RANGE: Northern Wyoming to California and northward. COMMENT: The common name, Lousewort, apparently comes from an early superstition that animals could acquire lice from the plants.

Figwort Family *(Scrophulariaceae)*

PINK FERNLEAF
Pedicularis contorta var. *ctenophora*
(Rydb.) N. & M. Although white or cream
colored flowers, often embellished with
purple spots, predominate in our alpine
flora, the pink or purplish variety shown
above occurs in some localities. RANGE:
Parts of Idaho, Montana, and Wyoming.

Figwort Family *(Scrophulariaceae)*

Figwort Family *(Scrophulariaceae)*

ELEPHANTHEAD

Pedicularis groenlandica Retz. These exquisite pink to magenta flowers unmistakably resemble elephants' heads. The upper petal, bulbous on top, imitates the animal's forehead and tapers into a long, narrow, gracefully curving trunk. Three lower petals spread wide to represent the ears and lower lip of the elephant. Many such flowers closely crowd the upper portions of unbranched stems. They stand 6 to 20 inches or more on reddish-purple stems and bear the pinnately lobed, fern-like leaves common to the genus. One finds these amusing beauties in the summer. HABITAT: Frequents wet meadows at subalpine and alpine altitudes. RANGE: Transcontinental in Canada and south through the Rockies and Cascades. COMMENT: A smaller species occurs in the southern Cascades and Sierras.

OEDER'S (ALPINE) LOUSEWORT

Pedicularis oederi Vahl. A dwarf version of Bracted Lousewort, but the end of the upper hood does not curve downward into a pointed beak. Note that the tip of the pistil may project out of the hood instead. These plants normally send up a single flowering stem, 2 to 8 inches tall. The leaves are pinnately lobed about ½ to ⅔ of the way to the midrib. The flowers originate in the axils of round leafy bracts shorter than the flowers. It blooms the first half of summer. HABITAT: Moist alpine meadows and tundra. RANGE: Circumpolar, south in the Rockies to Wyoming. COMMENT: Montana's rare species list includes this one.

Figwort Family *(Scrophulariaceae)*

Figwort Family *(Scrophulariaceae)*

PARRY'S LOUSEWORT

Pedicularis parryi Gray. Another alpine lousewort, 2 to 8 inches tall. The upper hood points downward in a pronounced beak, but does not curl or twist to the side. Crowded flowers, white, creamy, or yellowish, produce rather short inflorescences at the summit of the stem. The pinnately lobed leaves divide into narrow, toothed segments and sprout mostly from the base of the plant in a tuft. They bloom from June to August. HABITAT: Open rocky slopes and dry meadows, subalpine and alpine. RANGE: Southern Idaho and Montana to Arizona and New Mexico.

SICKLETOP LOUSEWORT, Parrot's Beak

Pedicularis racemosa Dougl. Unlike most louseworts this one produces simple, lance-shaped leaves, toothed on the edges and frequently copper toned. They attach mostly to the flower stem. The blossoms have sickle shaped upper petals that curve downward over a broad, 3-lobed lower lip. They resemble Coiled Lousewort, p. 96, but the leaves readily differentiate the two species. Also rather few in number, the flowers often tend to crowd near the top of the stem. White or cream colors predominate in our area, but pink ones do occur. The blooms open in summer. HABITAT: Woods in the higher mountains, mostly subalpine. RANGE: Common throughout most of the West.

Figwort Family *(Scrophulariaceae)*

ALPINE PENSTEMON, Mountain Beardtongue

Penstemon alpinus Torr. Lustrous blue, often tinged with pink or lavender, this penstemon commonly stands 8 to 16 inches high. Fairly close whorls of the flamboyant blooms tend to grow on one side of the upper half to ⅔ of the stem. Smooth green opposite leaves clasp the lower stem and extend upward into the floral arrangement, adding to the beauty of the plant. Blooms in summer. HABITAT: Gravelly slopes, most commonly subalpine, but also reaching alpine vistas to about 11,000 feet. RANGE: Southeastern Wyoming to New Mexico. COMMENT: Botanists have identified approximately 260 species of *Penstemon*, all but one of them native to North America.

Figwort Family *(Scrophulariaceae)*

Figwort Family *(Scrophulariaceae)*

ROCKVINE PENSTEMON

Penstemon ellipticus C. & F. Woody stems, like short vines, creep along the ground and over rocks, making rather dense mats. The bluish lavender flowers, 1 to 1½ inches long, possess prominent ridges along the tops of the floral tubes. The mouth of the tube opens wide to display hairy anthers within and a hairy lower lip. Small oval leaves (*ellipticus*) sometimes lightly toothed or indented, sit opposite on the stems. It blooms through the summer. HABITAT: Rocky places with some moisture, subalpine and alpine. RANGE: Montana and Idaho, north into Canada. COMMENT: A similar species, *P. davidsonii*, might be considered a variety of Rockvine Penstemon. It grows in the mountains of the west coast. Shrubby Penstemon, shown in Vol. II, *Forest Wildflowers*, could also be mistaken for this one.

MOUNTAIN PENSTEMON, Cordroot Penstemon

Penstemon montanus Greene. Several stems 4 to 12 inches tall rise in a cluster from a branching taproot crown. The leaves all grow on the stems, oval or lance shaped and toothed or with smooth margins depending on the variety. Gland-tipped hairs noticeably cover the stems, leaves, and the sharp lobes of the reddish-green calyces. These spectacular flowers grow opposite from upper leaf axils and one flower perches on the stem tip. Lavender to violet colors predominate on blossoms that are smooth on the outside with a distinct ridge on top and hairy within. Dense woolly hairs coat the anthers. July and August. HABITAT: Scree slopes and rock crevices, subalpine to alpine. RANGE: Western Montana and Wyoming to Idaho and Utah.

Figwort Family *(Scrophulariaceae)*

WHIPPLE'S PENSTEMON

Penstemon whippleanus Gray. This handsome penstemon grows in sparse clumps about 10 to 20 inches tall, the flowers openly whorled on unbranched stems. Colors of the flowers range from cream (with dark speckles) to wine, lavender, or purple. The lower lip of the blossom projects outward much farther than the upper and is quite hairy. Oval or lance-shaped leaves usually possess smooth edges. Look for it in mid- and late summer. HABITAT: Rocky hillsides with good drainage, mostly subalpine. RANGE: Eastern Idaho and S Montana and south through the Rockies.

Figwort Family *(Scrophulariaceae)*

Figwort Family *(Scrophulariaceae)*

CUSICK'S SPEEDWELL

Veronica cusickii Gray. Small intensely blue or violet flowers, ¼ to ½ inch across, composed of four petals irregular in size and spacing. The lower petal is conspicuously smaller than the other three. The style, a hairlike extension of the pistil, projects outward about ¼ inch, between two shorter stamens. Simple opposite leaves clasp the stems, but the leafy bracts of the inflorescence are alternate. These little beauties stand 2 to 8 inches high and spread by means of underground rhizomes. They bloom in midsummer. HABITAT: Wet meadows and moist hillsides at high altitude. RANGE: Western Montana to S British Columbia, NE Oregon and the Sierras.

AMERICAN ALPINE SPEEDWELL

Veronica wormskjoldii R. & S. This dark blue veronica possesses smaller flowers than *V. cusickii* and the styles and stamens do not project out as conspicuously. The blossoms develop into a rather tight, rounded head atop simple stems, 3 to 8 inches tall. Short hairs copiously coat the stems, while the leaves are usually smooth and sessile. Blooms occur in July and August. HABITAT: Subalpine and alpine. RANGE: Transcontinental in arctic and subarctic North America and south in the western mountains to New Mexico and California. COMMENT: Closely related *V. alpina* ranges from the arctic in NE North America to Europe.

SITKA VALERIAN, Mountain Heliotrope

Valeriana sitchensis Bong. Small white funnel-shaped flowers, pinkish in the bud, they crowd into rounded or hemispheric floral heads, 1 to 3 inches across. Five fused petals form the corolla tube and many stamens protrude from these arresting blossoms. Two or more pairs of opposite leaves attach mostly on the flower stems. They are pinnately compound, usually with 3 or 5 oval or lance shaped leaflets, the terminal leaflet the largest. Coarse shallow teeth mark the leaflet margins. The plants typically stand 1 to 3 feet tall and bloom from June to August. HABITAT: Moist ground on wooded slopes or meadows from mid montane to alpine. RANGE: Alaska to Montana and California. COMMENT: About six valerians, separable on technical characters, inhabit the Rockies.

Valerian Family *(Valerianaceae)*

Violet Family *(Violaceae)*

GOOSEFOOT VIOLET

Viola purpurea Kell. Splashy yellow violets show purple or brown guide lines on the lower petals and a purple tinge on the back of the upper petals. Variable leaf shape may be entire or roundly toothed. The leaves grow in a spreading clump, some or all starting from below ground and often tinged with purple and noticeably veined. The flowers open from May to August. HABITAT: Variable from montane to alpine scree slopes. RANGE: Montana to Colorado and Arizona and Washington to California.

Selected References

1. Booth, W.E. and J.C. Wright. *Flora of Montana, Part II*. Montana State Univ. Bozeman. 1959.

2. Clark, Lewis J. *Wild Flowers of the Pacific Northwest*. Gray's. Sidney, B.C. 1976.

3. Craighead, John J., F.C. Craighead and R.J. Davis. *A Field Guide to Rocky Mountain Wildflowers*. Houghton Mifflin. Cambridge. 1963.

4. Dittberner, P.L. and M.R. Olson. *The Plant Information Network (PIN) Data Base: Colorado, Montana, North Dakota, Utah and Wyoming*. U.S. Fish and Wildl. Serv. Washington. 1983.

5. Dorn, Robert D. *Vascular Plants of Montana*. Mountain West. Cheyenne. 1984.

6. Harrington, H.D. *Edible Native Plants of the Rocky Mountains*. Univ. of New Mexico. Albuquerque. 1976.

7. Hitchcock, C. Leo and A. Cronquist. *Flora of the Pacific Northwest*. Univ. of Wash. Seattle. 1973.

8. Hitchcock, C. Leo, A. Cronquist, M. Ownbey, and J.W. Thompson, eds. *Vascular Plants of the Pacific Northwest,* in 5 Vols. Univ. of Wash. Seattle. 1955 to 1969.

9. Lesica, P. *Checklist of the Vascular Plants of Glacier National Park*. Montana Acad. of Sci. 1985.

10. Lesica, P. *et al*. *Vascular Plants of Limited Distribution in Montana*. Montana Acad. of Sci. 1984.

11. Lyons, C.P. *Trees Shrubs and Flowers to Know in Washington*. Evergreen. Vancouver. 1956.

12. McDougall, W.B. and H.A. Baggley. *The Plants of Yellowstone National Park*. Wheelwright. 1956.

13. Moss, E.H. *Flora of Alberta*. Univ. of Toronto. 1959.

14. Nelson, Burrell E. *Vascular Plants of the Medicine Bow Range*. Jelm Mtn. Press. Laramie. 1984.

15. Nelson, Ruth A. *Handbook of Rocky Mountain Plants*. D.S. King. Tucson. 1969.

16. Niehaus, T.F. and C.L. Ripper. *A Field Guide to Pacific States Wildflowers*. Houghton Mifflin. Boston. 1976.

17. Roberts, H. and R. *Colorado Wildflowers*. Bradford-Robinson. Denver. 1959.

18. *Rocky Mountain Alpines*. Denver Botanic Gardens. Timber Press. Portland. 1986.

19. Shaw, R.J. and D. On. *Plants of Waterton-Glacier National Parks*. Mountain Press. Missoula. 1979.

20. Spellenberg, Richard. *The Audubon Society Field Guide to North American Wildflowers, Western Region*. Knopf. N.Y. 1979.

21. Taylor, R.J. and Spring, B. and I. *Rocky Mountain Wildflowers, Part 4*. Touchstone. Beaverton. 1978.

22. Weber, W.A. *Colorado Flora, Western Slope*. Colorado Univ. Press. Boulder, 1987.

23. Weber, W.A. *Rocky Mountain Flora*. Colorado Univ. Press Boulder. 1976.

Illustrated Glossary

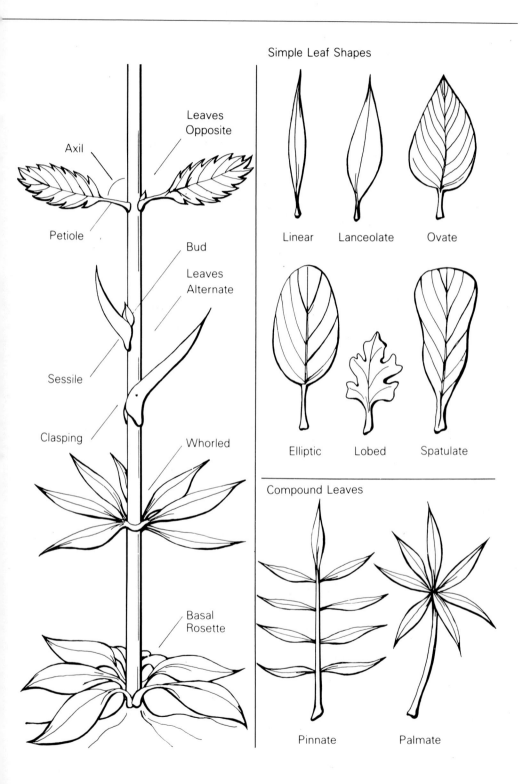

Simple Leaf Shapes

Axil

Leaves Opposite

Petiole

Bud

Sessile

Leaves Alternate

Clasping

Whorled

Basal Rosette

Linear   Lanceolate   Ovate

Elliptic   Lobed   Spatulate

Compound Leaves

Pinnate   Palmate

Glossary

Annual — A plant that completes its life cycle in one year.
Anther — The pollen producing appendage on the stamen.
Berry — A fleshy fruit containing seeds.
Biennial — A plant living for part or all of two years.
Bract — A leaf-like scale on a flower cluster.
Bulb — A plant bud usually below ground.
Calyx — The outermost portion of a flower, the sepals collectively.
Catkin — A dense spike or raceme with many scales and small naked flowers.
Clasping — As a leaf base surrounding a stem.
Column — A group of united stamens and pistils.
Corm — A bulb-like but solid underground swelling of a stem.
Disc flower or floret — Tubular flowers at the center of a composite head.
Drupe - A fleshy fruit with a stone-encased seed.
Gland — A spot or expanded area that produces a sticky substance.
Glaucus — Fine powder coating a surface.
Head — A cluster of flowers crowding the tip of a stem.
Hybrid — Pollination of a plant by another species or variety.
Inflorescence — An arrangement of flowers on a stem.
Irregular — Nonsymmetrical in shape or orientation.
Nectar — A sweet liquid produced by flowers that attracts insects.
Node — A point on a stem where leaves or branches originate.
Ovary — Part of the pistil containing the developing seeds.
Pedicel — The supporting stem of a single flower.
Peduncle — The stalk of an inflorescence or a single flower.
Perennial — A plant that lives more than two years.
Petals — The floral leaves inside the sepals.
Petiole — The stem supporting a leaf.
Pistil — The female organ of a flower.
Pollen — Masculine cells produced by the stamens.
Raceme — An inflorescence on a single stalk composed of flowers on pedicels.
Ray flowers or florets — Star-shaped flowers in a composite head.
Rhizome — A horizontal underground stem or rootstock.
Saprophyte — A plant that lives on dead organic matter.
Sepal — Outermost floral leaves, one segment of the calyx.
Serrate — Having short sharp teeth on the margin.
Sessile — Lacking a stem or pedicel, attached at the base.
Sheathed — Enclosing a stem at the base, clasping.
Shrub — A woody plant smaller than a tree.
Spathe — A large bract subtending or enclosing an inflorescence.
Spike — An inflorescence of sessile flowers on a single stalk.
Spur — A hollow appendage of a petal or sepal.
Stamen — The pollen producing organ of a flower.
Stigma — The end of the pistil that collects pollen.
Stolon — A horizontal stem from the base of a plant.
Style — The slender stalk of a pistil.
Succulent — Pulpy, soft, and juicy.
Tendril — A slender twining extension of a leaf or stem.
Tepals — Undifferentiated sepals and petals collectively.
Umbel — A group of stems or pedicels that arise from a common point on a stalk.
Whorl — Three or more leaves or branches growing from a node or common point.

Index

Achillea 16
Aconitum 70
Agoseris 16
Alkali Grass 13
Allium 10
Alpine Avens 81
Alpine Gold 24
Alp Lily 10
Alumroot 87
Androsace 67
Anemone 70
Antennaria 17
Apiaceae 14
Aquilegia . . . . 73, Front Cover
Arenaria 34
Arnica 18
Artemisia 18
Asphodel, False 11
Aster 19
Asteraceae 16
Astragalus 41

Beardtongue 100
Beargrass 12
Bellflower 32
Besseya 94
Biscuitroot 14
Bistort 63, 64
Bitterroot 66
Bladderwort Family 55
Bleeding Heart Family 46
Bluebell 28, 32
Borage Family . . . . 27, Back Cover
Bottle Brush 64
Brassicaceae 30
Bronze Bells 11
Buckwheat Family, Wild 61
Buttercup Family 70
Butterwort 55
Bupleurum 15

Caltha 76
Calyptridium 65
Campanula 32
Campion, Moss 36
Candytuft 31
Caryophyllaceae 34

Cassiope 38
Castilleja 92
Chaenactis 20
Chionophila 94
Cinquefoil 84
Cirsium 21
Claytonia 65
Clover 44
Collomia 58
Columbine . . . . 73, Front Cover
Compositae 16
Cornlily 13
Cowslip 76
Crassulaceae 37
Crazyweed 43
Cruciferae 30
Currant 52

Daisy 22
Death Camas 13
Delphinium 76
Dicentra 46
Dodecatheon 67
Dogtooth Violet 9
Draba 30
Dryas 80
Dusty Maiden 20

Elephanthead 98
Elk's Lip 76
Engelmann Aster 19
Epilobium 56
Ericaceae 38
Erigeron 22
Eriogonum 61
Eritrichium . . . . 27, Back Cover
Erysimum 30
Erythronium 9
Evening Primrose Family 56

Fabaceae 41
Fernleaf Sickletop 96
Figwort Family 92
Fireweed 56
Fleabane 22
Forget-Me-Not . . . . 27, Back Cover
Frasera 46

Fumariaceae 46

Gentian Family 46
Geum 81
Glacier Lily 9
Globeflower 77
Goldenweed 24
Gooseberry Family 52
Grass of Parnassus 88
Grossulariaceae 52
Haplopappus 24
Harebell Family 32
Heath Family 38
Hedysarum 42
Hellebore 13
Heuchera 87
Hulsea 24
Hydrophyllaceae 53
Hymenoxys 25
Hypericum 54

Indian Hellebore 13
Ivesia 81

Jacob's Ladder 60

Kalmia 38
Kelseya 82
King's Crown 37
Kittentails 94

Labiatae 54
Labrador Tea 39
Lanterns, Alpine 35
Larkspur 76
Laurel, Swamp 38
Ledum 39
Leguminosae 41
Lentibulariaceae 55
Lewisia 66
Lily Family 9
Linanthastrum 59
Lloydia 10
Locoweed 41
Lomatium 14
Lousewort 96
Luetkea 83
Lupinus 43
Lychnis 35

Marsh Marigold 76
Matvetch 41
Meadow Spiraea 83
Mertensia 28
Milkvetch 41
Mimulus 95
Mint Family 54
Monardella 54
Monkeyflower 95
Monkshood 70
Monument Plant 46
Moss Pink, Campion 36
Mountain Avens 80
Mountain Dandelion 17
Mountain Parsley 15
Mustard Family 30
Myosotis 28

Nailwort 35

Old Man of the Mountains 25
Onagraceae 56
Orange Agoseris 16
Orpine 37
Oxyria 63
Oxytropis 43

Paintbrush 92
Pale Agoseris 17
Papaveraceae 59
Parnassia 88
Paronychia 35
Parrot's Beak 99
Parsley Family 14
Partridgefoot 83
Pasqueflower, Western 71
Pea Family 41
Pedicularis 96
Penstemon 100
Petrophytum 83
Phacelia 53
Phlox Family 58
Phyllodoce 39
Pinguicula 55
Pink Family 34
Polemoniaceae 58
Polygonaceae 61
Poppy Family 59

Portulacaceae 65
Potentilla 84
Primrose Family 67
Primula 68
Pseudocymopterus 15
Purple Fringe 53
Purslane Family 65
Pussypaws 65
Pussytoes 17
Pygmy Bitterroot 66
Pygmy Poppy 59

Queen's Crown 37

Ranunculaceae . . . . 70, Front Cover
Ranunculus 78
Rhododendron 40
Ribes 52
Rock Fringe 57
Rock Jasmine 67
Rockmat 83
Rock Rose 57
Rose Crown 37
Rose Family 80
Roseroot 37

Sage 18
Salicaceae 85
Sandberg's Desert Parsley 14
Sandwort 34
Saussurea 26
Sawwort 26
Saxifrage Family 89
Scrophulariaceae 92
Sedum 37
Serpentgrass 63
Shooting Star 67
Sibbaldia 85
Siberian Chives 10
Sickletop Lousewort 99
Silene 36
Skunkleaf 60
Sky Pilot 60
Smelowskia 31
Snowlover 94
Sorrel 63
Speedwell 103
Spiraea 86

Spraguea 65
Spring Beauty 65
Star Felwort 51
Steer's Head 46
Stenanthium 11
Sticky Tofieldia 11
St. Johnswort 54
Stonecrop Family 37
Sunflower Family 16
Swamp Laurel 38
Sweetvetch 42
Swertia 51
Synthyris 94

Telesonix 91
Thistle 21
Thlaspi 31
Thoroughwax 15
Throughwort 15
Tofieldia 11
Townsendia 26
Trapper's Tea 39
Trifolium 44
Trollius 77

Umbelliferae 14

Valerian Family 104
Veratrum 13
Veronica 103
Violet Family 104

Wallflower 30
Waterleaf Family 53
Whitlowwort 35
Willowherb 56
Willow 85
Wood Betony 96

Xerophyllum 12

Yarrow 16

Zigadenus 13